D0860313

Efficient FORTRAN Programming

Efficient FORTRAN Programing

Anton Kruger

John Wiley & Sons, Inc.
New York / Chichester / Brisbane / Toronto / Singapore

Library of Congress Cataloging in Publication Data:

Kruger, Anton.
    Efficient FORTRAN programming / Anton Kruger.
      p. cm.
    Includes bibliographical references.
    1. FORTRAN (Computer program language)   I. Title.
QA76.73.F25K78   1990   90-12382
005.13'3—dc20   CIP
ISBN 0-471-52894-3

Printed in the United States of America

10 9   8 7 6 5 4 3 2 1

CONTENTS

PREFACE   **xi**

1 INTRODUCTION   **1**

2.1   Perspective on Efficiency 2
2.2   Measurements and Notation 4
2.3   The Programming Language 5
2.4   Algorithms and Implementations 6
2.5   Role of the Hardware 8
2.6   Data Structure 9
2.7   Role of the Compiler 13
2.8   When to Optimize 15
2.9   Summary 18

2 PROGRAMMING STRATEGIES   **19**

3.1   Simplicity-Speed Trade-off 20
3.2   Flexibility-Speed Trade-off 22
3.3   Use of Tables 24
3.4   Program Generation 28
3.5   Accuracy-Speed Trade-off 29
3.6   Narrowing the Scope of the Problem 31
3.7   Brute Force 33
3.8   Precomputing 34
3.9   Incremental Calculation 35
3.10 Memory-Speed Trade-off 39
3.11 Summary 39

3 MEASURING COMPUTING EFFICIENCY   **41**

4.1   Instrumentation of Programs 41
4.2   Manual Profiling 45
4.3   Coping with Optimization 49

4.4   Discussion   51

4   BASIC OPTIMIZATION   53

5.1   Constant Folding   53
5.2   Common Subexpression Elimination   54
5.3   Code Motion   54
5.4   Strength Reduction   55
5.5   Loop Combination   57
5.6   Loop Linearization   58
5.7   Character Strings   60
5.8   Boolean Expression Elimination   61
5.9   Use of Brackets   61
5.10   Avoiding Type Conversions   62
5.11   Statement Order and Data Interference   63
5.12   Side Effects   65
5.13   Summary   67

5   MEMORY MANAGEMENT   69

6.1   Virtual Memory and Page Faults   70
6.2   Overlay Linkers   72
6.3   Cache Memory   72
6.4   Referencing Memory   74
6.5   Array Initialization   76
6.6   Subroutines and Parameters   76
6.7   Declaring Variables   78
6.8   Memory Segmentation and Memory Models   79
6.9   Discussion   82

6   PROGRAM GENERATION   85

7.1   Inline Code   86
7.2   Inline Subroutine Calls   89
7.3   Threaded Code   90
7.4   Knotted Code   91
7.5   Inline Code Example   92
7.6   Threaded Code Example   95
7.7   Discussion   99

7   INPUT/OUTPUT   101

8.1   An Overview of File I/O   102
8.2   Formatted vs Unformatted I/O   103
8.3   Implied-Do Loop Collapsing   106
8.4   Run-Time Formatting   108
8.5   Data Reorganization   110
8.6   Data Reduction   111
8.7   I/O Buffer Size   112
8.8   System-Dependent Routines   114
8.9   Summary   114

8   GENERAL TECHNIQUES   **115**

   9.1   Intrinsic and Statement Functions 115
   9.2   Subroutine Libraries 116
   9.3   Language Extentions 116
   9.4   Assembly Language 121

9   EXAMPLE: POLYGON FILLING   **123**

   10.1   Some Definitions 123
   10.2   Flood Filling 124
   10.3   A Scan-Line Algorithm 125
   10.4   General Scan-Line Algorithm 126
   10.5   Data Structures 128
   10.6   Implementation 130
   10.7   Making the Edge Tables 131
   10.8   Updating the Edge Table Pointers 133
   10.9   Sorting the x-Intersections 134
   10.10 Drawing the Line Segments 135
   10.11 Discussion 136

10   EXAMPLE: FILE COMPRESSION   **137**

   11.1   Huffman Encoding 137
   11.2   Data Structures for the Huffman Tree 141
   11.3   I/O Routines 134
   11.4   The First Implementation 146
   11.5   Making the Symbol Frequency Table 147
   11.6   Building the Huffman Tree 149
   11.7   Writing the File Header 151
   11.8   Generating the Huffman Codes 151
   11.9   Packing the Code Bits 153
   11.10 Implementation of BTEST and IBSET 154
   11.11 A Profile of the Program 155
   11.12 Optimization: BTEST and IBSET_ 158
   11.13 Optimization: Buffered I/O 160
   11.14 Optimization: Look-Up Tables 165
   11.15 Decoding 169
   11.16 Discussion 171

11   EPILOGUE   **175**

REFERENCES   **177**

INDEX   **181**

PREFACE

This is a book about efficient FORTRAN programming. What is meant by the term *efficiency*? For the purposes of this book, it refers to execution, or run-time efficiency. Thus, if program A requires less time to perform the same function as program B, it is said to be more efficient than program B. One might ask: why a book on FORTRAN? It is an old language, but despite periodic predictions of its imminent death, FORTRAN is still going strong and, given the past accuracy (or lack thereof) of such predictions, will probably continue to do so for quite some time. For example, supercomputers are becoming increasingly important, and it is an irony that FORTRAN, and not some of the newer languages, is the dominant language on these computers. Other languages are available, but they are seldom supported to the degree that FORTRAN is on these machines. In any event, the vast majority of FORTRAN users do not work on supercomputers but on more traditional processors. It is this latter audience that is the target of this book. For the interested user there are some good texts on programming supercomputers [1].

Old age has its virtues, and because FORTRAN has been around for such a long time, many FORTRAN compilers are well refined, and armed with some knowledge of the compiler as well as the computer's hardware, it is possible to craft very efficient software in FORTRAN. In fact, Kernighan and Plauger use FORTRAN almost as an assembler for their *Software Tools* [2].

No language chauvinism is intended, however, and it is true that efficient programs can be written in, for example, PASCAL, C, and compiled BASIC. Many of the techniques discussed in this book apply equally to these languages, and where they do not, it is usually clear how the technique should be altered for a particular language. For instance, in Chapter 5 it is argued that if at all possible one should always vary the leftmost subscript of multidimensional arrays the fastest in FORTRAN, for this can lead to better execution time. This rule follows from the way FORTRAN stores multidimensional arrays, namely, column after column. For a language such as C, which stores arrays row after row, the rule becomes that the *rightmost* array subscript should be varied as fast as possible. Also, the program generation techniques discussed in Chapter 6 will work with any language. Thus, this book is by no means for FORTRAN programmers only.

Surprisingly few textbooks deal with the topic of programming efficiency. Those that do, usually do so in passing, and the reader is often left with the impression that efficiency is either not very important or not really under the control of the programmer. This is not true, of course, and the purpose of this book is to show how to program for efficiency, and that even simple alterations to existing programs can lead to dramatic reductions in execution time.

A serious attempt was made to show that optimization techniques are often hardware- and compiler-dependent. In order to do this, many example programs were timed on three computers, which included a Digital Equipment VAX and an Apollo engineering workstation. There was a time when bug-free FORTRAN compilers were nonexistent on microcomputers, but those days are fortunately gone. Today one can purchase full FORTRAN 77 optimizing compilers that also offer a wide range of common extensions found on mainframe computers. Personal computers are also becoming increasingly powerful, so that more and more scientists and engineers are using the PC as a major tool in program development. Indeed, in some instances the personal computer is used exclusively. Unfortunately, microcomputer FORTRAN users have been somewhat neglected in the literature. In this book, however, microcomputer FORTRAN is an integral part of the discussion. Two good compilers are the Lahey and the Microsoft compilers for MS-DOS personal computers, and they were used to time examples on an IBM microcomputer.

I would like to dedicate this book to my teacher, colleague, as well as friend, Mr. G.J. Kahl. He taught me much of what I value as an engineer, and also some about life, mostly by example.

ANTON KRUGER

Iowa City, Iowa
August 1990

Efficient FORTRAN
Programming

1

INTRODUCTION

Fashions come and go, and it is very hard to resist the temptation to be swept along with the current of popular agreement. It it nonetheless surprising to most nonscientists, and indeed many scientists, to discover that the supposedly hard, cold, and objective world of science does not escape trends. The fact is, science is as much prone to fashion as anything else. Despite some rumors to the contrary, scientists (which probably include computer programmers!) are human, so it is to be expected that some subjective viewpoints flourish and that a few emotions surface during scientific discourse.

The depth of some of these emotions are nevertheless surprising. Witness the response one recent letter on the infamous GOTO elicited [3]. Otherwise well-behaved, pondering scholars turned into sharp-witted, sometimes nasty correspondents. In fact, the editor had to step in, and in effect said "enough is enough." Writing letters to the editor almost turned into a blood sport!

Computing efficiency does not evoke quite the feelings that the GOTO statement does, but it is notwithstanding a contentious issue. It surely does not hold the position of importance that it did in the 1960s and early 1970s. At one point, some authors viewed the whole matter of efficiency almost with disgust, placing all emphasis on program structure and maintainability. Unfortunately this approach will often lead to rather inefficient programs, and most professional programmers and computer scientists now realize that there is more to programing than structure. The increasing popularity of microprocessors has certainly contributed to efficiency's new prominence. Also, much research has gone and still goes into better (which very often means more efficient) algorithms.

1

1.1 PERSPECTIVE ON EFFICIENCY

Why is run-time efficiency important? First, in most cases a programmer has an account and is charged for use of the resources of the computing facility. This includes CPU time, and the adage *Time Is Money* is applicable. Second, some engineering and scientific problems are so complex that straightforward implementations of standard algorithms will result in execution times that are prohibitively long. Thus new methods are needed to solve these problems. Another reason is that some tasks simply need to be done as fast as possible. Examples include real time image processing, many computer graphics applications, interactive computer-assisted design, and so forth.

Computing resources are constantly becoming cheaper. Some of the personal computers available today rival minicomputers of a few years ago. Random access memory (RAM), improved CPUs, and mathematics and graphics coprocessors that add to the power of computers have become relatively cheap. On the other hand, the cost of *programming* computers has not decreased. This must be taken into account when optimization is considered. Modern compilers often have a multitude of options, of compiler switches, that can be specified when compiling a program. By simply using these options prudently, one can often speed up a program considerably.

It is valid to ask whether it is worthwhile spending a lot of (expensive) programming time on a routine that will be used only a few times. Also, does it make economic sense to painstakingly optimize a long and complex program when the same improvement in execution performance can be had with better hardware, or even a newer version of the FORTRAN compiler?

To make the discussion more concrete, consider the Figure 1.1, which is based on information taken from [4]. The figure shows the relative execution times for a specific benchmark, namely LINPACK. Each bar represents the execution time for a specific version of the Lahey FORTRAN compiler. Shown above each bar are the compiler options used for the measurement. Note in particular the difference in execution time for the same program compiled with version 3.01 of the Lahey compiler and version 4.0 of the compiler. As the graph shows, one can almost cut the running time of the program in half just by upgrading the compiler.

Now consider the next example. Say a subroutine takes 10 msec to execute, and assume that an hour's coding effort reduces the execution time to one-tenth of this value, i.e., 1 msec. This an order of magnitude improvement, which is nothing to sneeze at. To be worth the investment in programmer time, however, the subroutine must be executed at least $(60 \times 60)/0.01 = 360,000$ times to break even. One hour of programmer time may also be more expensive that one hour running time on the computer, so the routine may need to be executed much more than 360,000 times to make financial sense.

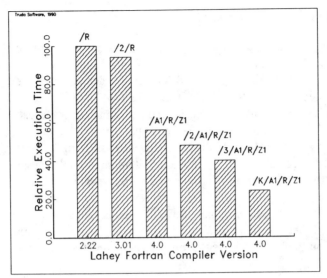

Figure 1.1: Lahey FORTRAN Compiler Version vs Relative Execution Time.

On the other hand, "bottom-line" arguments such as these are often very misleading and shortsighted, for many salient points are missed. For example, to effectively optimize a program often requires thorough knowledge of the problem statement, operating environment, computer hardware, as well as the computer language, which in the case of this book is FORTRAN. A programmer may spend what seems to be an inordinate amount of time optimizing a specific subroutine, but the knowledge and experience gained in this endeavor are often applied to other, analogous problems. What initially looks like a waste of time may therefore turn out to be a wise investment in the long run.

Thus, one can see that efficiency is a multifaceted aspect of computer programming. This book does not purport to settle these issues. It is implicitly assumed here that the different questions have been dealt with by the programmer, and attention is focused on the *process* of writing efficient FORTRAN programs.

Several steps are involved in the process of writing efficient programs, some of which include:

- Choice of the programming language
- Choice of an algorithm/data structure for the problem at hand
- Taking computer hardware into account
- Taking the compiler characteristics into account
- Actual coding or implementation of the algorithm

These and related issues are discussed in some the following sections.

1.2 MEASUREMENTS AND NOTATION

Before getting to the business of efficient computing, some comments on the notation used in the book are in order. First, FORTRAN, and standard FORTRAN in this book refer to FORTRAN 77, described in the American National Standards Institute (ANSI) X3.9-1978 standard. Though the example programs by and large adhere to this standard, some language extensions are used for the sake of clarity. For example, just about all implementations of FORTRAN support an INCLUDE statement in some form or another, so the programs of Chapters 9 and 10 use this statement to make program listings shorter and clearer. Sometimes variable and routine names longer that six characters are used.

Second, the example programs are set in a different type from that of the text. The "!" inline comment character is also widely available on many compilers, and is used to clarify code, but arrows are also sometimes used:

```
PROGRAM DEMO
INTEGER    I,K
REAL       X(5000),Y(5000) <────── Note the dimensions are 5000
           .
           :
X(I) = 2.0*I
CALL ARRADD(X,Y,5000)           ! Add 5000 data points
K = Y(I)
           .
           :
STOP
END
```

This example also shows how vertical ellipsis is used to indicate missing code.

Many examples listed in the book were timed, usually on three computers. The first is a VAX 11/780 running version V4 of its compiler. This is a solid compiler that is used for serious number crunching. The second is an Apollo DN4000, and this machine is representative of so-called engineering workstations. The Apollo has good graphics capabilities, a good FORTRAN compiler, and uses a Motorola MC68020 processor. The DN4000 unit used included an MC68881 floating-point coprocessor. The programs were also timed on an IBM PS/2 model 30 microcomputer, which has an 8086 processor, 640K RAM, and a sluggish (80 msec) hard disk. The system also has an 8087 coprocessor. Two compilers were used on the microcomputer, namely, Lahey version 2.0, and Microsoft version 4.01. (Both companies have released newer versions of their products.) The Lahey compiler requires a coprocessor, but the Microsoft compiler has an option that enables the user to use or ignore a coprocessor if one is present. For further details on these computers, the compilers, and the various compiler options, the reader should refer to the proper compiler manuals.

The results of measurements are usually displayed in a table similar to the one below:

Compiler	t_{power}/t_{normal}
Apollo	2.17
$MS_{(NO87)}$	0.34
$MS_{(87)}$	2.41
Lahey	2.12
VAX	1.5

One column lists the compilers for which the example was timed; the other lists the timings made as a ratio of the execution time of two routines. One routine is usually normal, unoptimized FORTRAN, and is used as the reference. The other routine is an attempt to improve execution speed for the routine. The table above, for example, shows that the optimized routine POWER (whatever that may be) in reality improved execution speed in only one instance, that of the $MS_{(NO87)}$ compiler.

"Apollo" in the table refers to the Apollo Domain compiler running on the Apollo DN4000 engineering workstation. Unless stated otherwise, all programs on the Apollo were compiled with the -OPT 4 (full optimization) compiler switch set. "$MS_{(NO87)}$" refers to the Microsoft version 4.01 compiler, the program compiled with the /Ox /FPc compiler switches set, and the NO87 environment variable on the IBM PS/2 model 30 microcomputer set. This means that full optimization is performed but that the coprocessor is not used during program execution. Instead calls to a floating-point library are performed. "$MS_{(87)}$" also refers to compilation with the /Ox /FPc switches set, but now the NO87 environment variable is not set. This means that a coprocessor is used. If the presence or absence of a coprocessor has no influence on execution speed, the same options were used to compile the programs, but then the compiler is shown as "Microsoft" in the table.

If a program was tested on the Lahey compiler, it is listed as such in the table. The options used to compile the programs are:

$$/NA /B /NL /NS$$

The meaning of these options are /NA: adjustable arrays can be larger than 65,280 bytes; /B: bound checks array subscripts and adjustable dimensions; /NL: no line number table; /NS: do not generate debugging information. Finally, "VAX" in the table refers to programs run on the VAX compiler, compiled with the all the default options, which include full optimization, and no debugging information generated.

1.3 THE PROGRAMMING LANGUAGE

Computer languages are designed to accomplish specific tasks, and although certain languages are flexible enough to be used in many different applications, it is usually best to use the proper language for a particular problem. In any event, this book is about efficient FORTRAN programming, so it is implicitly assumed that this book addresses FORTRAN-specific programming problems.

1.4 ALGORITHMS AND IMPLEMENTATIONS

In his excellent book *Programming Pearls* [5], Jon Bentley gives an example of how a "lowly" Radio Shack TRS-80 model III microcomputer running an interpreted BASIC search program outperforms a FORTRAN search program on a Cray-1 supercomputer. The reason for this anomaly is that the BASIC program implemented an inherently efficient algorithm. Even though the *implementation* and execution of the algorithm on the Cray computer was very efficient and "state of the art," the *algorithm* was inefficient. This underscores the importance of an algorithm in a dramatic way, for little can surpass a good algorithm. A similar argument holds true for data structures, and the choice of a proper data structure can have a major influence on the complexity and efficiency of a program.

One can implement a particular algorithm efficiently and ensure that the hardware runs at full capacity, or by poor coding offset much of the gain that a good algorithm provides. For example, the loops in both (a) and (b) below initialize an array, but the code in (a) is faster than the code in (b). On the Apollo workstation, for example, (a) took 13.7 sec to complete, and (b) took 71 sec, or about five times longer to complete.

```
        REAL   X(1024,1024)              REAL   X(1024,1024)

        N = 1024                         N = 1024
        DO 20 J = 1,N                    DO 20 I = 1,N
           DO 10 I = 1,N                    DO 10 J = 1,N
              X(I,J) = J                       X(I,J) = J
10         CONTINUE              10         CONTINUE
20      CONTINUE                 20      CONTINUE
        STOP                             STOP
        END                              END

            (a)                              (b)
```

The only difference between (a) and (b) lies in the order in which the array indices are varied. What a dramatic difference for such a small change! The reason for this difference in execution speed is discussed in Chapter 5. This simple example should make the point clear — the implementation and coding of an algorithm does matter.

Now consider the computation of the discrete Fourier transform (DFT). The DFT is an important tool in digital spectrum analysis and has found extensive use in many different fields. It is used in this book as a vehicle to illustrate some of the points made. The importance of the DFT is due mainly to the 1965 publication of an efficient algorithm for the computation of the DFT [6]. This special computational procedure, known as a *radix-2* fast Fourier transform (FFT) algorithm, can be used to compute the DFT. FFT algorithms are not restricted to radix-2, but radix-2 algorithms are quite efficient and by far the most common. Actually, the basic algorithm seems to have been used long before 1965, and Heideman [7] credited the mathematician Gauss with its invention. This by no means negates the importance of the 1965 paper, and since the algorithm's "rediscovery," many related algorithms have been developed, and all of these are collectively referred to as fast Fourier transforms.

In any event, the DFT of a sequence of numbers $x(n)$, $0 \le n \le N$ is defined as

$$X(k) = \sum_{n=0}^{N-1} x(n)e^{-j(2\Pi/N)nk} \qquad k = 0, 1, \ldots, N-1$$

and $x(n)$ may, in general, be complex. From this equation it follows that to compute each $X(k)$, N complex multiplications and $N-1$ complex additions must be made. Since there are N such $X(k)$'s, the total number of complex multiplications are N^2, and the total number of complex additions are $N(N-1)$ ($\approx N^2$ for large N). For large values of N the number of operations to compute the DFT may become prohibitive.

If the number of data points in the sequence $x(n)$ is a power of 2, one can use Cooley's radix-2 algorithm to compute the DFT, which requires $(N/2)\log_2 N$ complex multiplications. The next table shows N^2 and $(N/2)\log_2 N$ for a various N.

N	N^2	$(N/2)\log_2 N$
8	64	12
16	256	32
32	1024	80
64	4096	192
128	16,384	448
256	65,536	1024
512	262,144	2304
1024	1,048,576	5120

For 128 data points the FFT has $16,384/448 = 36$ times fewer multiplications, and for 1024 data points about 200 times (more than two orders of magnitude) fewer! It is safe to say that no amount of "fine tuning" of a program implementing the DFT directly can lead to this kind of savings. The actual implementation of the FFT algorithm can take on a number of different forms. In a following chapter, for instance, the program generation technique is applied to the implementation of a FFT algorithm. This can result in FFT programs that are much faster than the normal, straightforward implementation of the FFT algorithm.

1.5 ROLE OF THE HARDWARE

High-level computer languages free the programmer from a computer's under-lying hardware. A programmer can, in principle at least, submit a valid FORTRAN program to the compiler on any system and expect identical output. This is seldom true in practice, as anyone who has attempted to port a program from one compiler to another can attest. Apart from different "features" or language extensions that compiler manufacturers build into their compilers, one often finds that implementations of the supposedly FORTRAN standard differ from one compiler to another. The accompanying portability issue is an impor-tant one but is not the topic of this book, although some reference will be made to it.

Differences between computers have another side too, and this is very much pertinent to the topic of program efficiency. For instance, to improve execution speed, a subroutine that makes heavy use of the intrinsic SIN function can be coded to (a) set up a table of sines on the first call and (b) on any subse-quent calls look up sine values in the constructed table. This is a valid approach if the sine function is calculated in software. That is, each call to the SIN function in the source program is compiled as a call to a math subroutine library. Even with the math subroutine library coded in the host computer's machine language, a table look-up method will probably be faster than recalcu-lation of the needed sines.

On the other hand, if the system hardware includes a numeric processor, and the compiler generates instructions that make use of this, the SIN function will be computed in hardware, which can be many times faster than equivalent software routines [8]:

> Coprocessors are the least expensive and easiest way to increase the numerics performance of a small computing system. In the simplest case, the owner of an IBM PC AT can buy an Intel 80287, say, and simply plug it into a socket on the main board. The immediate result is to speed up— perhaps by 100 times— the mathematical operations of software that has been compiled to include a few special instructions of the math processor.

Also, a table look-up method increases program size and, as will be shown later, program size and execution speed are not necessarily mutually independent. Because of this, look-up tables might even reduce execution speed in some instances.

This example clearly shows that the system hardware can have an influence on the implementation strategy. Here, the presence or absence of special hard-ware dictated the use of look-up tables or direct calculation of the SIN function. Other aspects, such as memory layout and management, word size, and so forth, also have an important bearing on execution time and are discussed in later chapters.

1.6 DATA STRUCTURE

Below is a program that reads 2000 words from a file, sorts the words, and then writes the sorted list to another file. The sorting is done by a subroutine SORT, which is an implementation of Shell's sort algorithm. This algorithm is often used for sorting $N = 100$ to 2000 data points, because it is quite simple to program, and with a worst case execution time proportional to $N^{3/2}$ [9], not too expensive.

```
      PARAMETER          (NW = 2000)
      REAL               TE1,T1,T2
      CHARACTER*30       CARR(NW),CWORK
      PARAMETER (ALN2I=1.4426950, TINY=1.E-5)

C Read file to sort.
      OPEN(1,FILE='UNSORTED')
      DO 10 I = 1,NW
         KEY(I) = I
         READ(1,'(A)')CARR(KEY(I))
   10 CONTINUE
      CLOSE(1)

C Sort.
      LOG2N = INT(ALOG(FLOAT(NW))*ALN2I+TINY)
      CALL SORT(CARR,NW,LOG2N,CWORK)
      OPEN(1,FILE='SORTED')
      DO 20 I = 1,NW
         WRITE(1,'(A)')CARR(I)
   20 CONTINUE
      CLOSE(1)
      STOP
      END
                              (a)


      SUBROUTINE SORT (CARR,N,LOG2N,ITEMP)
C Sorts the character array CARR with Shell sort algorithm.
      CHARACTER*(*)      CARR(*),ITEMP

      M = N
      DO 30 NN = 1,LOG2N
         M = M/2
         K = N - M
         DO 20 J = 1,K
            I = J
   10       L = I + M
            IF (LLT(CARR(L),CARR(I))) THEN
               ITEMP   = CARR(I)
               CARR(I) = CARR(L)
               CARR(L) = ITEMP
               I       = I - M
               IF(I.GE.1) GOTO 10
            ENDIF
   20    CONTINUE
   30 CONTINUE
      RETURN
      END
                              (b)
```

Exchange elements if necessary

Any sort algorithm must have a *compare function* that decides when one element lies ahead of another (or is bigger, smaller, etc.) in the desired order. The compare function in SORT is the code:

```
(LLT(CARR(L),CARR(I)))
```

where LLT is the FORTRAN *Lexically Less Than* function. The ASCII character set is used, regardless of the host computer's collating sequence. This means that LLT('A','a') is .TRUE., because capital letters precede lower case letters in the ASCII set, and also that LLT('a','Z') is .FALSE. If the following list in (a) is sorted with the compare function above, the list in (b) will result:

art	Art
bee	More
Art	Zinc
zero	art
rest	bee
More	rest
Zinc	zero
(a)	(b)

Refer back to the program, and note that each field (word) in the array that must be sorted can have a maximum of 30 characters. In all, 3 x 30 = 90 characters (bytes) are copied from one location to another for each swap that occurs. This is time consuming, and becomes worse when larger fields are used. By arranging the data slightly differently, this problem can be circumvented. An integer array can be used as an array of pointers to the elements that must be sorted. This array is called the *key* array of the data. For the previous list of words, the keys will look like this before sorting:

CARR(1) = art	;	key(1) = 1,	= >	CARR(key(1)) = art
CARR(2) = bee	;	key(2) = 2,	= >	CARR(key(2)) = bee
CARR(3) = ART	;	key(3) = 3,	= >	CARR(key(3)) = ART
CARR(4) = zero	;	key(4) = 4,	= >	CARR(key(4)) = zero
CARR(5) = rest	;	key(5) = 5,	= >	CARR(key(5)) = rest
CARR(6) = More	;	key(6) = 6,	= >	CARR(key(6)) = More
CARR(7) = Zinc	;	key(7) = 7,	= >	CARR(key(7)) = Zinc

The keys are passed along with the data array to the sort function. The basic algorithm stays the same, but now the keys are used instead of the elements of the data array. The compare function becomes:

```
(LLT(CARR(KEY(L)),CARR(KEY(I)))),
```

and when this is .TRUE., the keys are swapped. After sorting the keys, they should look like this:

CARR(1) = art   ;   key(1) = 3,   => CARR(key(1)) = ART
CARR(2) = bee   ;   key(2) = 6,   => CARR(key(2)) = More
CARR(3) = ART   ;   key(3) = 7,   => CARR(key(3)) = Zinc
CARR(4) = zero ;   key(4) = 1,   => CARR(key(4)) = art
CARR(5) = rest ;   key(5) = 2,   => CARR(key(5)) = bee
CARR(6) = More ;   key(6) = 5,   => CARR(key(6)) = rest
CARR(7) = Zinc ;   key(7) = 4,   => CARR(key(7)) = zero

The keys are integers (typically 4 bytes wide), so that $3 \times 4 = 12$ bytes are copied for each swap, which is much less than the original 90 bytes. The time it takes to swap should be dramatically less and will also not depend on the field width of the data array. (The time to compare two elements will of course still depend on the width.) The next program implements these ideas:

```
      PARAMETER          (NW = 2000)
      CHARACTER*30       CARR(NW),CWORK
      INTEGER            KEY(NW)
      PARAMETER          (ALN2I=1.4426950, TINY=1.E-5)

C Read the file to sort.
      OPEN(1,FILE='UNSORTED')
      DO 10 I = 1,NW
         KEY(I) = I          <———— Initialize keys
         READ(1,'(A)')CARR(KEY(I))
   10 CONTINUE
      CLOSE(1)

C Sort.
      LOG2N = INT(ALOG(FLOAT(NW))*ALN2I+TINY)
      CALL SORTKY(CARR,NW,LOG2N,KEY)   <———— Sort keys of CARR
      OPEN(1,FILE='SORTED')
      DO 20 I = 1,NW
         WRITE(1,'(A)')CARR(KEY(I)) <———— KEY(I) points to next element
   20 CONTINUE
      CLOSE(1)

      STOP
      END
                                    (a)



      SUBROUTINE SORTKY (CARR,N,LOG2N,KEY)
C Sort the character array CARR with Shell sort
C algorithm. Sort keys rather than array itself.
      CHARACTER*(*)     CARR(*)
      INTEGER           KEY(*)
      INTEGER           ITEMP
C
      M = N
      DO 30 NN = 1,LOG2N
         M = M/2
```

```
      K = N - M
      DO 20 J = 1,K
         I = J
10       L = I + M
         IF ( LLT(CARR(KEY(L)),CARR(KEY(I))) ) THEN
            ITEMP    = KEY(I)
            KEY(I)   = KEY(L) ───┐
            KEY(L)   = ITEMP  ───┴────── Exchange keys if necessary
            I        = I - M
            IF(I.GE.1) GOTO 10
         ENDIF
20    CONTINUE
30    CONTINUE
C

      RETURN
      END
```

(b)

The new program is very similar to the original one. It requires slightly more memory, for each element of the data array has a key associated with it. The increase in efficiency is substantial, as the next table shows. It lists the ratio of execution speed of the key sort subroutine and the normal sort when sorting 2000 words randomly selected from an English dictionary. On the microcomputer the key sort took roughly a third less time to complete than the normal sort. On the other computers the reduction is even greater — on the Apollo it takes only 40% as long to perform the sort.

Compiler	$t_{\text{key sort}}/t_{\text{normal}}$
Apollo	0.40
Microsoft	0.62
Lahey	0.78
VAX	0.51

The normal sort, as well as the key sort, employs the same Shell sort algorithm, but the key sort subroutine used a different data structure, that of an array of pointers to manipulate the data. It is this new data structure that eliminated a lot of needless copying of data from one location to another. This in turn resulted in dramatic improvement in execution speed in some instances.

This example clearly shows how a proper data structure can improve execution speed. Standard FORTRAN does not have data structures such as records, or explicit pointers, but this should not exclude their use in programs. All the important data structures — arrays, records, lists, stacks, queues, and so on, — can be implemented in FORTRAN, admittedly sometimes not as clearly as in other languages, but implemented nonetheless. For example, it is common to use linear arrays to hold sparse multidimensional arrays (arrays with many zero elements), and this can save space, but also reduce execution time [10]. As another example, lists and graphs are often used in computer graphics [11].

1.7 ROLE OF THE COMPILER

In the previous section it was argued that program code must to some extent be adapted to the computer's underlying hardware. The same is true for the type (or even version) of compiler used on the system. Microcomputer magazines often publish reviews in which different compilers are "squared off" against each other. All kinds of benchmark programs are used to compare execution times of compiled programs, and from this the potential buyer can decide which compiler to purchase. Apart from producing "winners", these contests highlight an important point — not all compilers are created equal. A well-written program should produce correct results if compiled on the same system with different compilers. Execution speed, however, often differs greatly.

This has implications for the programmer, for a programming technique that results in a major improvement in performance on one compiler may give no or only marginal improvements with another. Many of the examples in this book will illustrate this fact. While it may be possible for microcomputer users to shop around to find the fastest compiler, other programmers usually have to accept the compiler on their system as a given.

It might not be the most exciting thing in the world to do, but valuable hints on how to improve a program's performance can often be found in the compiler's user's guide. (Unfortunately, this documentation is not always readily available to programmers, and if it is available, it is seldom current.) For example, the PRIME computer's FORTRAN manual suggests that the order in which a program's subroutines are loaded has an influence on the execution speed and that the most frequently called routines must be loaded first. It is not always clear which routines are used most frequently, but if it is, one should heed the manufacturer's advice.

As another example, the Apollo Domain FORTRAN manual recommends declaring array arguments in subroutines with dimension 1 to improve execution speed:

```
      PROGRAM DEMO
      REAL   X(5000),Y(5000) <—— Note the dimensions are 5000
            .
            :
      CALL ARRADD(X,Y,5000)
            .
            :
      STOP
      END


      SUBROUTINE ARRADD(X,Y,N)
      REAL       X(1),Y(1) <—— Note the dimensions are 1
      DO 10 I = 1,N
         X(I) = X(I) + Y(I)
   10 CONTINUE
      RETURN
      END
```

The true dimensions of the arrays X and Y are 5000, but the declared dimensions in the subroutines are 1. While not standard FORTRAN, the Apollo FORTRAN compiler turns off array subscript checking with such a declaration. Usually this compiler produces code that generates error messages if a subroutine attempts to reference arrays outside their actual boundaries. This takes time, and by turning subscript checking off, execution speed is enhanced. Whether it is wise to turn off subscript checking is another matter, for exceeding array bounds is a quite common source of errors. On the other hand, is has been argued by some authors, subscript checking can safely be turned off for well-written, correct programs. What is important here, however, is that on many other compilers the above program will produce either errors during compilation or run-time errors. Thus, a technique that improves execution speed on one compiler may generate errors on another, especially if nonstandard language features are used.

Most compilers come with a variety of *compiler switches* or options through which the user can control any number of aspects of the code that the compiler generates. The compiler switches commonly instruct the compiler to:

- Turn on/off array subscript bounds checking
- Generate inline code for certain functions
- Generate code for a specific CPU
- Optimize to specific levels
- Use an integer word size, i.e., INTEGER*2, or INTEGER*4
- Control floating-point operations
- Use certain memory models (on microcomputers)

Compiler options are important because they can have a dramatic effect on the performance of a program, and in some cases without influencing portability of a program. On the 8086 family of microprocessors, which have a word size of 2 bytes (16 bits), it is much more efficient to use 2-byte (INTEGER*2) instead of 4-byte (INTEGER*4) integers, but the penalty is that integer variables are limited to range from -32,767 to 32,767. On other machines such as the IBM 370, use of the INTEGER*2 switch usually degrades performance, for they have a 4-byte hardware integer architecture, and when the user specifies INTEGER*2, it cannot fully optimize all operations and address calculations.

Consider next the subroutine SORT which sorts an array of integers stored in IARR, and takes the arguments N (number of data points) and LOG2N ($=\log_2 N$):

```
      SUBROUTINE SORT (IARR,N,LOG2N)
      INTEGER    IARR(N)
C
      M = N
      DO 30 NN = 1,LOG2N
        M = M/2
        K = N-M
```

```
        DO 20 J = 1,K
            I = J
10          L = I+M
            IF (IARR(L) .LT. IARR(I)) THEN
                ITEMP    = IARR(I)
                IARR(I) = IARR(L)
                IARR(L) = ITEMP
                I        = I-M
                IF(I.GE.1) GOTO 10
            ENDIF
20      CONTINUE
30      CONTINUE
        RETURN
        END
```

It is a slight variation of the SORT subroutine of Section 1.6. In an application where a large number of data sets are sorted repeatedly, one might want to reduce execution time, and it is logical to consider other algorithms, e.g., Quicksort. Alternatively, one can first experiment with compiler switches and try to improve performance that way. If the data points lie between -32,767 and 32,767, one can use INTEGER*2 instead of INTEGER*4 integers by setting an appropriate compiler switch. Here are the results for sorting 5000 (random) integers:

Compiler	$t_{INTEGER*2}/t_{INTEGER*4}$
Apollo	~1
Microsoft	0.52
Lahey	0.65
VAX	1.29

The table shows that a simple compiler switch can make an important difference, and in this case improved the performance by almost two times on microcomputer. However, on both the Apollo and the VAX, performance went down, so the converse is also true: the improper use of compiler switches can degrade performance. The good thing about compiler switches is that they provide a very convenient way of experimenting with a program without making changes to the program itself. Returning to the increased performance on the microcomputers, in many cases the improvement might be sufficient and no alterations to the program are needed. If execution time is still a problem, other algorithms must be considered. It should be clear, however, that proper use of compiler switches is a powerful tool in achieving program performance.

1.8 WHEN TO OPTIMIZE

On practically all computers integer multiplication is more expensive (time consuming) than integer addition. Thus, the code in (a) below can be made more efficient by replacing J = 2*J with J = J+J. In doing so, one would replace 100 multiplications with 100 additions. For (b) one could again use J = I+I instead of J = 2*I. In the latter case, however, J is not calculated in a loop, and in the interest of readability one should opt to leave the code as it is. In makes little sense to alter perfectly legal, readable code in parts of a program where little can be gained.

```
      DO 10 I = 1,100                          I = 20
            .                                       .
            .                                       .
            .                                       .
         J = 2*J                              J = 2*I
   10   CONTINUE

          (a)                                      (b)
```

Modern compiler theory (and many previous FORTRAN compilers) enables compiler writers to create extremely good compilers. In fact, some compilers optimize so efficiently that even good programmers would be hard pressed to do better. Simple optimizations are best left to the compiler, and the programmer's time can in many cases best be spent in improving the algorithm or data structure. One must identify time consuming parts of a program and optimize those. Often a few critical lines are all that need to be changed. It is important to find these bottlenecks, do alterations there, and leave the rest as is. In other words: *If it ain't broke, don't fix it!* Chapter 3 takes a look at methods of finding the "hot spots" in a program.

Optimization should be done only on working code and correct algorithms, and several authors have made the point: do not optimize too early [12],[13]. On the other hand, while some optimization techniques are pretty dramatic, others are simple, common sense rules which quickly become part of a programmer's writing. Applying the latter while coding can help a lot to improve execution speed, and they can be used "on the fly."

A classic example of misplaced emphasis on efficiency is the generation of random numbers. Random numbers are used in applications such as simulation and Monte Carlo integration. Since these applications are often very time consuming, there is a need for methods that can generate random numbers fast. By far the most widely used method is the *multiplicative linear congruential* method. The principle is quite simple. Two constants a and m are chosen, and then the recursion

$$z_{n+1} = MOD(az_n, m)$$

and a suitable starting z (called the seed) will give a sequence of pseudo-random numbers. For example, with $a = 3$, $m = 7$, and the initial seed 1, the sequence is 1, 3, 2, 6, 4, 5, 1 .... Note that the period of the sequence is $m - 1 = 6$, so m should be as large as possible so as to maximize the period of the random sequence. The algorithm is misleadingly simple, especially if one starts to consider efficiency. Because the MOD function really implies a division, one can improve the speed of the generator by performing an efficient integer division, which often means dividing by a factor of 2 (see Section 8.3). Also, one can reduce execution time by speeding up computation of the product *az*. Again, if *a* is a factor of 2, it will usually be faster. These ideas gave rise to a some fairly "efficient" routines, but according to Stephen Park and Keith Miller [14]:

> ... programmers who knew more about code optimization than random number generation concentrated on the development of multiplicative generators with non-prime moduli of the form $m = 2b$ where b was matched to the integer word size of the computer. The primary reason for this was execution speed. With a suitable choice of the multiplier *a* and some low-level programming the *az* product could be reduced to several shifts and adds and the mod *m* operation could be accomplished by *controlled* integer overflow. The result of this emphasis on speed was a generation of computational efficient but highly non-portable and statistically flawed multiplicative linear congruential generators, the most notorious being the now infamous IBM SYSTEM/360 product *RANDAU*.

The RANDAU random number generator was used for many years, and Park and Miller list a large number of programming texts that still include flawed multiplicative linear congruential random number generators.

The purpose of a random number generator is exactly that: to generate a sequence of numbers that is statistically as random as possible. The constants *a* and *m* must therefore be chosen primarily in order to produce a sequence with the best statistical properties, and not for efficient implementation. The moral, then, is that efficiency should never compromise correctness.

Instead of leaving the reader in suspense on good values for *a* and *m*, intensive research [15] has limited the number of possibilities considerably, and $a = 16807$ for $m = 2^{31} - 1 = 2147483647$ seems to be a fairly good choice. Park and Miller take this as a minimal standard random number generator, and discuss implementation considerations. Next is a FORTRAN version of the minimal standard:

```
REAL FUNCTION RAND(ISEED)
INTEGER    A,Q,R
INTEGER    HI,LO
INTEGER    TEST
PARAMETER  (A=16807, M=2147483647, Q=127773, R=2836)

HI  = ISEED/Q
LO  = MOD(ISEED,Q)
TEST=A*LO-R*HI
IF(TEST .GT. 0) THEN
  ISEED=TEST
ELSE
  ISEED=TEST+M
ENDIF
RAND=REAL(ISEED)/REAL(M)
RETURN
END
```

This implementation is portable and correct on systems that use at least 32-bit integer arithmetic, i.e., integers are 4 bytes wide, and can represent numbers that range from -2147483647 to +2147483647. The function RAND returns a real number that lies between 0.0 and 1.0. The theory behind the algorithm is described by Park and Miller, and they also suggest the next program to test for a correct implementation:

```
      ISEED=1
      DO 10 I=1,10 000
         U=RAND(ISEED)
   10 CONTINUE
      WRITE(*,*)ISEED
      STOP
      END
```

The program should produce the number 1043618065. This is by no means the last word on random number generators, and readers who wish to learn more about the topic should consult Park and Miller's paper; it contains a wealth of valuable references on the subject.

1.9 SUMMARY

The purpose of this chapter was to give an overview of the issues that have a bearing on computing efficiency. Because it is the topic of this book, it is easy to lose perspective and get the impression that efficiency is the only concern in program development. It is not. Books are limited by their format to using relatively short and easy examples in explanations. Program clarity and maintainability, therefore, do not take on their proper importance. Real-life computing applications are often very complex, and may involve many programmers. Because more than one programmer may work on a piece of code, either during development or in later modifications, program clarity and modularity are often of greater concern than execution speed in all but the most critical parts of a program. Similar arguments hold for portability.

All this having been said, efficiency is an important consideration in a large number of applications, and many factors contribute to an efficient program. Not all factors are under the control of a programmer, but this does not mean that a programmer should not be concerned with them. On the contrary, some knowledge of the hardware, for instance, is desirable, for it can influence a programming strategy.

2

PROGRAMMING STRATEGIES

Probably everyone has played the guessing game in which one player picks an object and the other has to guess what the object is. People invariably play the game for what it is— a guessing game. They pick an object at random and then see if it is correct. Another way of playing the game is to ask in which half of the room the object is located. On getting the response, one asks in which half of the remaining half, then in which half of the remaining quarter, and so on. With 10 questions one can limit the location of the object to a volume $1/2^{10}$ of the total volume of the room. For an average room this would be a volume small enough to then locate the object.

What was done here was restating of the particular problem of *guessing* the location of an object to one of *searching* for an object. By restating the problem, the random unorganized method of locating the object was transformed into a simple iterative procedure for searching. In fact, a standard way of searching an ordered list of items is to do a so-called binary search, and the basic principle stays the same: the list of items is divided into two, and one half is searched. If the item is not found, the remaining half is again divided, and one half searched. The whole procedure is repeated until the item is found.

The point is this: there is usually more than one way of looking at a problem, and more than one programming strategy probably exists for solving a particular task. While modern computers can perform calculations at truly remarkable speeds and handle astounding amounts of information, their capacity is not unlimited. For some computing tasks the resources available do seem unlimited, and straightforward programming methods will suffice. Other problems quickly deplete resources if standard approaches are followed, and in these instances innovative methods are needed. In this chapter attention is paid to some of the different techniques that can be used to accomplish a task.

2.1 SIMPLICITY-SPEED TRADE-OFF

Below is a string conversion routine ATOI1 that accepts a character string as an argument and returns an integer. The string is assumed to hold the character representation of an integer, e.g., STRING =' -123'. The function ATOI1 returns the value of the string, so that 2*ATOI1('51') is the number 101.

```
      INTEGER FUNCTION ATOI1(STRING)
      CHARACTER*(*)    STRING
      CHARACTER*5      FMT

      DO 10 L = LEN(STRING),1,-1
         IF (STRING(L:L) .NE. ' ') GOTO 20
  10  CONTINUE
  20  FMT = '(I   )'
      WRITE(FMT(3:4),'(I2)')L
      READ(STRING,FMT)ATOI1
      RETURN
      END
```

The operation of ATOI1 is straightforward. The DO loop determines the nonblank length of the character variable STRING by scanning it backward until the first nonblank character is found. Upon exit from the loop, the variable L is the required length. The next two statements generate a format specifier FMT. If L were, for instance, 10, FMT would be FMT = '(I10)'. Finally, the conversion from a character string to integer is made by treating STRING as an internal file, and reading its value into ATOI1.

ATOI1 is clear, concise, and just about as flexible as the host compiler's internal conversion routines, for that is what is in effect being put to use in this function. The character string can contain leading as well as embedded blanks; ATOI1 will correctly perform the conversion. Since the format specifier FMT cannot exceed FMT = '(I99)', the maximum nonblank length of the character string should be less than 99. A signed 4-byte integer variable can take on values that range from -2,147,483,647 to +2,147,483,647, so strictly speaking, only 11 digits are needed. Since the character string may contain leading and embedded blanks, however, up to 99 characters are allowed in this version of ATOI1. (It is difficult to imagine situations where this will not be sufficient.)

An important aspect of ATOI1 is that it is portable. It does not depend on any peculiarities of a compiler, or on the compiler's character-collating sequence. So ATOI1 seems to be a bargain— simple and portable. But there is a hidden cost. FORTRAN's READ and WRITE instructions must be able to perform all format conversions — characters, real numbers, complex numbers, list-directed input/output, etc. Because they must cater to all possibilities, they are fairly large and slow.

Next is another string conversion routine, called ATOI2. A statement function ISDIGT is defined inside ATOI2 and, as its name suggests, it returns .TRUE. If its argument is a digit, ATOI2 skips over the leading blanks, then it scans for a '-' or a '+' character to determine the sign. The last part of the program scans the character string until no more digits are found. If a character representation of a digit is found, it is converted to an integer, multiplied with the proper factor of 10, and added to the answer.

```
      INTEGER FUNCTION ATOI2 (STRING)
      CHARACTER*(*)   STRING
      CHARACTER*1     C
      INTEGER         I, S
      LOGICAL  ISDIGT <------- ISDIGT returns .TRUE. if argument is a digit
      ISDIGT(C) = (LGE(C,'0') .AND. LLE(C,'9'))

C Skip over leading blanks, and determine sign.
      ATOI2 = 0
      I     = 1
10    IF (STRING(I:I) .EQ. ' ') THEN
         I = I + 1
      GOTO 10
      ENDIF
      S = 1
      IF (STRING (I:I) .EQ. '+' .OR. STRING (I:I) .EQ. '-') THEN
         IF (STRING(I:I) .EQ. '-') S = -1
         I = I + 1
      ENDIF

C Convert.
20    IF (ISDIGT (STRING(I:I))) THEN
         ATOI2 = 10*ATOI2 + ICHAR(STRING(I:I)) - ICHAR ('0')
         I = I + 1
      GOTO 20
      ENDIF
      ATOI2 = S*ATOI2
      RETURN
      END
```

As it is, ATOI2 does not allow embedded blanks. It stops conversion on the first nondigit found, but it is fairly easy to alter ATOI2 to allow for embedded blanks. Since ATOI assumes that the host compiler uses the ASCII collating sequence, the statement:

```
      ATOI2 = 10*ATOI2 + ICHAR(STRING(I:I)) - ICHAR ('0')
```

will not produce the required results on computers that do not use the ASCII character set. So ATOI2 is not as portable as ATOI1.

The next table shows the relative execution time for the two string conversion routines on the Apollo workstation, the PC running Microsoft FORTRAN, and the VAX. The measured times correspond to the execution time for converting the character string '+1234567890'. In all cases ATOI2 is much faster. ATOI2 is not really complicated but is certainly not as simple as ATOI1; however, the simplicity of ATOI1 also made it slow. As an added bonus, it turns out that despite its longer source code, ATOI2 actually produces substantially smaller executable object files (see Section 2.10).

Compiler	t_{atoi2}/t_{atoi1}
Apollo	0.15
Microsoft	0.21
VAX	0.22

2.2 FLEXIBILITY-SPEED TRADE-OFF

A subroutine that calculates the DFT from its definition (see Section 1.4) is shown below. The exp(-j2πnk/N) term was expanded according to Euler's formula:

$$e^{-j2\Pi nk/N} = \cos(2\Pi nk/N) + j\sin(2\Pi nk/N)$$

and several small changes in notation were made. The sequence to be transformed is stored in the array X, and upon return from the subroutine, array Y contains the DFT of the sequence of numbers. The variable NP is the length of the data sequence.

```
      SUBROUTINE DFT(X,Y,NP)
      COMPLEX      X(NP),Y(NP)
      PARAMETER    (PI = 3.1415926)
C
      DO 20 N = 1,NP
         Y(N) = 0.0
         DO 10 M=1,NP
            ARG  = (2.0*PI*(N-1)*(M-1))/NP
            Y(N) = Y(N)+X(M)*CMPLX(COS(ARG),-SIN(ARG))
   10    CONTINUE
   20 CONTINUE
      RETURN
      END
```

A radix-2 FFT algorithm [16] to calculate the DFT is shown next. The input sequence is again in array X, but the output is returned in X, whereas the previous subroutine left the input data intact. In many cases one need not preserve the input data, so that the second program would lead to a storage saving of N complex data points. This becomes important when very large data sequences must be transformed.

```
      SUBROUTINE FFTA (X,N,M)
      COMPLEX X(N),U,W,T
      PI = 3.141592653589
C Bit reversal.
      NV2 = N/2
      NM1 = N-1
      J   = 1
      DO 7 I = 1,NM1
         IF (I.GE.J) GOTO 5
```

```
              T     = X(J)
              X(J) = X(I)
              X(I) = T
    5         K     = NV2
    6      IF (K.GE.J) GOTO 7
              J = J-K
              K = K/2
           GOTO 6
    7      J = J+K

C Main part of FFT.
        DO 20 L = 1,M
           LE  = 2**L
           LE1 = LE/2
           U   = (1.0,0.)
           W = CMPLX(COS(PI/LE1),SIN(PI/LE1))
           DO 20 J = 1,LE1
              DO 10 I = J,N,LE
                 IP   = I+LE1
                 T    = X(IP)*U
                 X(IP) = X(I)-T
   10            X(I)  = X(I)+T
   20   U = U*W
        RETURN
        END
```

It was argued in Section 1.4 that for 1024 data points, about 200 times fewer multiplications are needed for the FFT than a direct computation of the DFT. If multiplication is the most expensive operation, then the FFT should be at least 200 times faster than the DFT. The next table shows t_{DFT}/t_{FFT}, where t_{DFT} is the time taken to compute the DFT directly and t_{FFT} is the time to compute the DFT via the FFT algorithm. Measurements were done on the Apollo DN4000 workstation.

N	t_{DFT}/t_{FFT}
256	80
512	141
1024	258

For 1024 complex data points the FFT turns out the be about 260 times faster than the DFT on the Apollo, and this reduction can best be appreciated by running the two programs. The FFT takes about 0.7 sec — a (slow) blink of the eye. The DFT takes a little over 3 min. The penalty for this performance improvement is longer and more complex code.

Since the particular FFT algorithm is radix-2, it is limited to transforming data sequences that have lengths that are powers of 2, while the direct implementation of the DFT has no such restriction. To gain even more speed, other FFT algorithms such as radix-4 or even radix-8 FFTs provide some performance improvement over radix-2 FFTs, but not nearly as dramatic as the radix-2 over a direct DFT algorithm. Improved performance comes at even less flexibility, for radix-4 FFTs require the lengths of data sequences to be powers of 4 and, in the case of radix-8 algorithms, powers of 8. In some applications these limitations do not matter, but in others they do. In such cases one has several options.

The first and most common is to *pad* the input data with a number of zeros to get the proper length. As an example, say the input consists of 60 points. Padding the data with four zeros gives a length of $2^6 = 64$ points, and a radix-2 FFT algorithm can be used. The disadvantage is that the transform of the new sequence is not the transform of the original one, and it must be interpreted properly to get the original transform. What if the number of data points is 10,000? The next power of 2 is 16,384, and if one were to pad with zeros, it would mean appending 6384 zeros. This has implications for memory usage as well as for efficiency, for padded data points are also transformed, even though they are not part of the actual data.

Another alternative is to use more general FFT algorithms. Singleton, for example, wrote a very efficient *mixed radix* FFT program [17] which can (in principle) transform data sequences of arbitrary length. The price paid for this versatility is program size and complexity, for Singleton's routine consists of about 500 lines of FORTRAN, with 90 GOTO statements, about 60 statement labels, and is not what one would consider casual reading.

2.3 USE OF TABLES

One way to improve execution speed, often dramatically, is to create a table that holds data that a program uses frequently. For example, consider the factorial function $n! = (1)(2)...(n-2)(n-1)n$. The computation of this function requires $(n-1)$ nontrivial multiplications. The subroutine in (a) below implements a straightforward calculation of the factorial from its definition, and the routine in (b) is an implementation that uses a small table to holds the first 11 values of n!

```
      REAL FUNCTION FACT(N)
      FACT=1.0
      DO 10 I=2,N
         FACT=FACT*I
10    CONTINUE
      RETURN
      END
```

```
      REAL FUNCTION FACT(N)
      REAL TABLE(0:10)
      DATA TABLE /1,1,2,6,24,120,
     +            720,5040,40320,
     +            362880,3628800/

      IF (N.LE.10) THEN
         FACT=TABLE(N)
         RETURN
      ENDIF
      FACT=TABLE(10)
      DO 10 I=11,N
         FACT=FACT*I
10    CONTINUE
      RETURN
      END
```

(a)   (b)

For n equal or less than 10, $n!$ is simply looked up in the table, saving $(n-1)$ multiplications. If n is greater than 10, $n!$ is calculated as $n! = 10!(11)(12)...(n-1)(n)$, saving nine multiplications. Assume that array indexing (table look-up) for small arrays is much faster than multiplication, so that execution time is proportional to the number of multiplications. Thus, the table version should compute 33! in about $(33-9)/33 = 73\%$ of the time it takes the subroutine in (a) to compute 33! The table below summarizes the improvement in execution speed of the table version of the factorial function over the direct calculation. The execution times were measured for 33! and correlate roughly with the expected values.

Compiler	t_{table}/t_{normal}
Apollo	0.69
$MS_{(NO87)}$	0.71
$MS_{(87)}$	0.72
Lahey	0.78
VAX	0.74

Now consider another, more extended, application. Digital images are often processed by convolving them with certain matrices. With a proper choice of the matrix, it is possible to filter the image, do edge detection, and so on. Figure 2.1 shows the procedure for a 3 x 3 convolution matrix **M**:

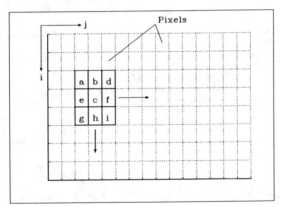

Figure 2.1: Convolving a Matrix with an Image.

The center of the 3 x 3 matrix **M** is moved from pixel to pixel in the image. At each pixel, the sum of the product of the nine elements in the matrix and the pixels they cover become the value of the center pixel in a derived image. Thus if P_1 denotes the original and P_2 the derived image, the next relation holds:

$$
\begin{aligned}
P_2(i,j) \quad = \quad & a*P_1(i\text{-}1,j\text{-}1) \quad + \quad b*P_1(i\text{-}1,j) \quad + \quad d*P_1(i\text{-}1,j+1) \\
+ \quad & e*P_1(i\ ,j\text{-}1) \quad + \quad c*P_1(i\ ,j) \quad + \quad f*P_1(i\ ,j+1) \\
+ \quad & g*P_1(i+1,j\text{-}1) \quad + \quad h*P_1(i+1,j) \quad + \quad k*P_1(i+1,j+1)
\end{aligned}
$$

The matrix **M** need not be 3 x 3, but most often it is, for while larger matrices may give better results, they also involve more computation. To compute a new pixel with the 3 x 3 matrix takes nine multiplications and eight additions, but usually some relation holds between the coefficients *a, b, c, d, e, f, g, h,* and *i*. A typical matrix might look like this:

$$M = \begin{bmatrix} a & b & a \\ b & c & b \\ a & b & a \end{bmatrix}$$

That is, there are only three different coefficients in the matrix. Next is a program fragment that performs the convolution on a 128 x 128 image, held in the two-dimensional array P1. For the sake of brevity the code that reads the image into P1, and later displays the new image, was omitted.

```
      PROGRAM    2D
      INTEGER    P1(128,128)
      INTEGER    P2(128,128)
      INTEGER    A,B,C

      A  = 1
      B  = 2
      C  = 3
      NX = 128
      NY = 128

C Perform Convolution.
      DO 50 J = 2,NX-1
         DO 40 I = 2,NY-1
            P2(I,J) = ( A*P1(I-1,J-1)+B*P1(I-1,J)
     +            +    A*P1(I-1,J+1)+B*P1(I,J+1)
     +            +    A*P1(I+1,J+1)+B*P1(I+1,J)
     +            +    A*P1(I+1,J-1)+B*P1(I,J-1)
     +            +    C*P1(I,J) )
40          CONTINUE
50    CONTINUE

      STOP
      END
```

Symmetry can be exploited to reduce the number of multiplications and additions. The first two terms on the left-hand side of the expression:

$$P_2(i,j) = a*P_1(i\text{-}1,j\text{-}1) + b*P_1(i\text{-}1,j) + \cdots$$

correspond to the two pixels indicated below:

$$M = \begin{bmatrix} \underline{a} & \underline{b} & a \\ b & c & b \\ a & b & a \end{bmatrix}$$

Say the number of gray levels in the digital image is 4. That is, $P_1(i,j)$ can take on the values 0, 1, 2, and 3. The sum of the first two terms can then take on any of $4 \times 4 = 16$ values, that range from $0, a, 2a, 3a, a+b, a+2b \ldots 3a+3b$. These possible values can be stored in a two-dimensional table:

$$\text{TABLE}(i,j) = \begin{bmatrix} 0 & b & 2b & 3b \\ a & a+b & a+2b & a+3b \\ 2a & 2a+b & 2a+2b & 2a+3b \\ 3a & 3a+b & 3a+2b & 3a+3b \end{bmatrix}$$

Instead of calculating $a*P_1(i-1,j-1) + b*P_1(i-1,j)$, it is simply looked up in the table:

$$a*P_1(i-1,j-1) + b*P_1(i-1,j) = \text{TABLE}(P_1(i-1,j-1), P_1(i-1,j))$$

The same table can also be used for the other pixels which must be multiplied with the coefficients a and b. The next program implements these ideas, with NG the number of gray levels and TC a separate table for the center pixel.

```
        PROGRAM    2DTAB
        INTEGER    P1(128,128)
        INTEGER    P2(128,128)
        INTEGER    TABLE(64,64)
        INTEGER    TC(64)
        INTEGER    A,B,C

        A = 1
        B = 2
        C = 3
        NX = 128
        NY = 128
        NG = 64

C Set up tables.
        DO 20 J = 1,NG
          DO 10 I = 1,NG
            TABLE(I,J) = I*A+J*B
10        CONTINUE
20      CONTINUE
        DO 30 I = 1,NG
          TC(I) = I*C
30      CONTINUE

C Perform Convolution.
        DO 50 J = 2,NX-1
          DO 40 I = 2,NY-1
            P2(I,J) = ( TABLE(P1(I-1,J-1),P1(I-1,J))
     +               +  TABLE(P1(I-1,J+1),P1(I,J+1))
     +               +  TABLE(P1(I+1,J+1),P1(I+1,J))
     +               +  TABLE(P1(I+1,J-1),P1(I,J-1))
     +               +  TC(P1(I,J)) )
40        CONTINUE
50      CONTINUE

        STOP
        END
```

Below is t_{table}/t_{normal}, the ratio of execution time of the two programs, for various compilers:

Compiler	t_{table}/t_{normal}
Apollo	1.43
$MS_{(NO87)}$	0.42
$MS_{(87)}$	0.42
Lahey	0.79
VAX	~1

This data illustrates two important points. First, the use of tables did not enhance performance on all computers. Second, different compilers on the same hardware (Microsoft and Lahey on a microcomputer) produced substantially different results. The reason for the differences lies in the relative weight of array indexing and mathematical operations for a particular compiler. In the case of the Microsoft compiler, address calculations needed for indexing the table take much less time than multiplications and additions. Thus, replacing them with table look-up proves very effective and reduces execution time an impressive $1/0.42 = 2.4$ times. The same holds for the Lahey compiler, but the improvement is less. However, on the Apollo, address calculations needed for the table method, as well as the fetching of data from memory, are more expensive than the multiplications and additions it attempts to prevent, and performance goes down.

In some applications one knows beforehand that all elements of a table are going to be used, and in these applications it makes sense to compute all values at the outset. The DFT and FFT programs listed in Section 2.2 are examples of this. In many other applications only certain values in a table are used on a specific run of the computer program. If the whole table is initialized, a lot of computing time is wasted, for many entries will never be looked up. In these applications it is best to evaluate table entries only as they are needed and then store them in the table for future use. This is called *lazy evaluation*.

2.4 PROGRAM GENERATION

A program generator is a program that has as output not numbers on a line printer, or a graph on a terminal, but another program. A compiler can be considered a program generator since it produces a machine language program as output. In this book the term is used more restrictively, and it refers to a FORTRAN program that produces another FORTRAN program. The generator program takes as input certain parameters and during execution produces another FORTRAN program, often in text file format. The generated program is then compiled and executed to produce the final results. A schematic diagram of the process is shown in Figure 2.2.

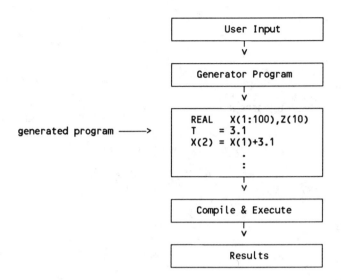

Figure 2.2: Schematic Diagram of Program Generation.

The motivation behind the method is that a "general" program that caters to all the possibilities of a particular problem is often not as efficient as a tailor-made program. For example, the loop indices in the FFT algorithm discussed earlier are only a function of the length of the data sequence. For an application where repeated calls are made to the subroutine with fixed data lengths, a special subroutine that eliminates computation of loop indices can be written to compute the FFT, and this subroutine will be more efficient than the regular FFT implementation.

Instead of hand-coding such a subroutine, a program is written to perform this task. The generator program accepts the length of a data sequence and produces a special FFT subroutine for that specific length. The generated subroutine is then incorporated into a main program. Several variants of program generation exist and are discussed in more detail in Chapter 6.

2.5 ACCURACY-SPEED TRADE-OFF

Consider the program below. It consists of main program DRIVER, a nonlinear function TEST, and a function ROOT [18]. The purpose of ROOT is to find the root of a function that is assumed to lie in the interval e_0. ROOT is called with the function FUNC(X) (TEST in this case), the two limits X1 and X2 of the interval e_0, a variable EPS, and lastly a variable N. The root is refined until its accuracy is known within $\pm$ EPS. While not usually included in such functions, the variable N here returns the number of iterations needed for convergence of ROOTS.

```
PROGRAM DRIVER
EXTERNAL TEST

EPS = 0.1
WRITE(*,*)'    EPS         N'
DO 10 K = 1,7
    EPS = EPS/10.0
    R   = ROOT(TEST,-1.5,-2.5,EPS,N)
    WRITE(*,'(1X,1P,E8.2,I6)')EPS,N
10  CONTINUE
END
```

(a)

```
REAL FUNCTION TEST(X)
TEST = X**2.0+5.0*X+6.0+TAN(0.1*X)
RETURN
END
```

(b)

```
FUNCTION  ROOT(FUNC,X1,X2,EPS,N)
EXTERNAL  FUNC
PARAMETER (MAXITR = 40)

FMID = FUNC(X2)
F    = FUNC(X1)
IF (F.LT.0.) THEN
    ROOT = X1
    DX   = X2 - X1
ELSE
    ROOT = X2
    DX   = X1 - X2
ENDIF
DO 10 J = 1,MAXITR
    N = J
    DX   = DX*0.5
    XMID = ROOT + DX
    FMID = FUNC(XMID)
    IF (FMID.LE.0.) ROOT = XMID
    IF (ABS(DX).LT.EPS .OR. FMID.EQ.0.) RETURN
10  CONTINUE
WRITE(*,*)'ERROR: ROOT DID NOT CONVERGE'
END
```

(c)

The main program calls ROOTS with different values for EPS, then prints the number of iterations needed for convergence for that particular EPS. Here is the output from the program:

```
   EPS       N
1.00E-02    8
1.00E-03   11
1.00E-04   14
1.00E-05   18
1.00E-06   21
1.00E-07   24
1.00E-08   28
```

Many engineering calculations need only be accurate to, say, two or three decimal places, and by stopping the iteration soon enough one can save computing time. For instance, if a root of this function needs to be known to only 1E-3, but ROOTS is called with EPS = 1E-6, it can take almost twice as many iterations to obtain the desired root. The number of iterations needed for convergence was measured here, but one can in some cases make a fairly accurate estimate if one knows a little bit about the algorithm employed.

The function ROOT shown above determines the root with the *bisection* method. Given an interval e_0 in which the root of the function is assumed to lie, the bisection method evaluates the function at its midpoint (hence the name) and at the two limits of the interval. The interval limit which gives the same sign as the midpoint is then replaced by the midpoint, and the procedure is repeated. The interval is thus halved on each iteration. Figure 2.3 illustrates this process.

The number of iterations needed to come within a distance e of the root is readily seen to be:

$$n = \log_2 e_0/e$$

For instance, in the previous example ROOTS was called with X1 = -1.5 and X2 = -2.5, so the initial interval e_0 is -1.5-(-2.5) = 1, and for a desired convergence interval e = 1E-7, $\log_2 e_0/e$ is equal to 23.25 or 24 iterations. This corresponds to the measured number of iterations, for this e at least. For other values it might be slightly different, depending on the particular function and rounding error.

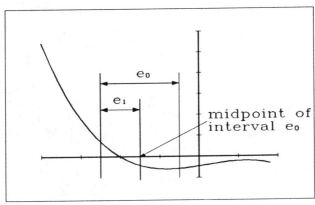

Figure 2.3: The Bisection Method.

2.6 NARROWING THE SCOPE OF THE PROBLEM

Routines that must perform a variety of functions are often slow. Consider the problem of computing the number x^n, that is, raising a real number x to the n-th power. The simple FORTRAN statement Y=X**N, will perform the computation. But the compiler has to allow for all possibilities: X real, X integer, N real, N negative, etc. In an application where only integer powers are needed, one might consider replacing $Y = X**N$ with a special routine.

There are several algorithms for evaluating integer powers, and the *right-to-left binary exponentiation* algorithm below is described by Knuth [19]. The algorithm computes *power* $= x^n$, where n is a positive integer.

Step 1: Set *power* $= 1, Z = X, N = n$
Step 2: Set $N = N/2$, and determine if N was even. If N was even, go to step 5.
Step 3: Set *power* $= Z*power$.
Step 4: If $n = 0$, the algorithm terminates, and *power* $(= x^n)$ is the answer.
Step 5: Set $Z = Z*Z$, and go to step 2.

The following function is a FORTRAN implementation of the algorithm. The statement labels correspond to the steps of the algorithm, and the program variable NN corresponds to the algorithm variable N. K is a temporary variable to hold NN's previous value.

```
      REAL FUNCTION POWER (X,N)
C Function returns X**N with X real, N integer > 0
C
   1    NN    = N
        POWER = 1.0
        Z     = X
   2    K = NN
        NN = NN/2
        IF ((K-2*NN).EQ. 0) GOTO 5
   3    POWER = POWER*Z
   4    IF (NN .EQ. 0 ) RETURN
   5    Z = Z*Z
      GOTO 2
      RETURN
      END
```

The only part of the function that needs some explanation is the statements:

```
         :
         :
   2    K  = NN
        NN = NN/2
        IF ((K-2*NN).EQ. 0) GOTO 5
         :
         :
```

If NN = 12 (even), then K = 12, NN becomes 6, and K-2*NN = 0. If NN is odd, say, 13, then K becomes 13, NN becomes 13/2 = 6 (remember: FORTRAN integer division), and K-2*NN becomes 1. So the IF statement becomes .TRUE. if NN is even, and .FALSE. if odd, and is step 2 of the algorithm. The multiplication by 2 in the IF statement is not really costly. Integer multiplication by 2 can be accomplished by shifting the bit pattern to the right one place. For more on this, and on other methods of testing for odd or even integers, refer to Section 8.3.

The next table summarizes the ratio of the execution speed for the routine POWER above, and the statement $Y = X**N$, with $N = 30$. On the computers with floating-point support available, the routine did not achieve its goal. On the Apollo, on the VAX, and on the microcomputers with a coprocessor present, it increased execution time. But on the microcomputer with no coprocessor present, POWER reduced execution time dramatically.

Compiler	t_{power}/t_{normal}
Apollo	2.17
$MS_{(NO87)}$	0.34
$MS_{(87)}$	2.41
Lahey	2.12
VAX	1.5

2.7 BRUTE FORCE

What's in a name? *Brute force*, quick-and-dirty, etc., refer basically to the same thing. Whether one likes it or not, brute force is used in practically all fields of human endeavor, and programming is no exception. Some problems call for elegant solutions, others for careful design, while some problems are best solved by what are euphemistically called *maximum effort techniques.*

In control theory, for example, one brute force technique is referred to as *bang-bang* control. A heat-seeking missile has flaps to control its flight, and with bang-bang control, the system will steer by switching flaps in either one of two positions. In other words, it will go bang-bang between the two positions. Bang-bang control systems often prove very effective, being fast, cheap, and also relatively easy to design. The academically inclined among us might feel guilty about using muscle instead of brains. It should be a consolation, therefore, to know that the theory of optimal control shows that for some problems, the maximum effort (brute force) solution to a particular problem is also the optimal solution. To bring the concept of brute force into the realm of programming, consider the following [20]:

> Sometimes brute force is not only simpler than intelligence, but more efficient as well. A case in point is the painter's algorithm, one of the oldest techniques for rendering three-dimensional images on computer screens. It solves the hidden-surface problem— how not to draw a section of an object that is obscured by objects in front of it — by ignoring the difficulty.
>
> The painter's algorithm avoids the problem by rendering a scene onto the screen from back to front (most distant objects first, closest objects last). This way, closer objects obscure more distant ones without any complicated hidden-surface calculation.

This hints at the two reasons for using brute force techniques, namely, it can be fast or it can be simple. Indeed, in some cases brute force may be a fast as well as simple solution to a particular problem, and the painter's algorithm is a case in point. This is not to say that good programming practices should be abandoned. On the contrary, all of the options available, including brute force, should be taken into consideration before deciding on a solution.

2.8 PRECOMPUTING

Generating realistic computer images involves a considerable number of computations. For a 1024 x 1024 pixel image, with 6 bytes/pixel (2 bytes per primary color), a total of 6MB of data per frame is needed. Apart from the normal process of clipping, projection, and transformation to generate a computer image, the realistic rendering of such images relies on some sort of shading model to account for the effects of light on the scene. Shading models can take diffuse reflection, ambient light, specular reflection, and shadows into account. All this adds to the computational burden.

Given this background, the generation of an animation scene (even a short one) seems like a formidable task, and this is indeed the case. One technique for dealing with this is to do as much precomputing as possible. In a wide variety of computer graphics applications it is only the viewpoint of the observer that changes; the world stays the same. An engineer might want to interactively rotate and get different views of a machine part being designed on a computer-aided design (CAD) system. Pilots using a flight simulator to practice repeated landings at the same airport is another example. In these cases where the environment is static, all the possible scenes can be precomputed and displayed as needed. All the computer does in real time is to determine, in response to user input (through a joystick, for instance), which scene must be displayed, then display the scene by reading the image from disk into the computer's video display buffer.

Actually, the process is not that simple, for to calculate all possible scenes would require an infinite amount of memory. Instead, the image is broken down into a large number of polygons that make up the picture. The list of polygons that make up a scene is called a *polygon list*. The polygon list can be viewed as an image database. To generate a specific scene the polygon database must be accessed and the picture can be generated. Describing a computer image in terms of a database is common in computer graphics, and is an example of the importance of a data structure. The precomputation technique takes advantage of the static environment and preprocesses the database once, for all possible cases. With the right preprocessing technique reasonable results can be obtained.

2.9   INCREMENTAL CALCULATION

Consider the situation where the squares of consecutive integers are needed. The next loop will calculate the first NSQ squares as the variable ISQ.

```
      DO 10 I = 1,NSQ
        ISQ = I*I
10    CONTINUE
```

Because the squares are computed in order, it is possible to speed up the calculations markedly. Next are the first five squares and their first order differences, as well as their second order differences:

Squares:	1	4	9	16	25
First order differences:		3	5	7	9
Second order differences:			2	2	2

The second order differences are constant (2), so one can calculate a square with addition from the previous square and the previous difference. The next piece of code uses this principle to perform the same function as the loop above. The variable IDIFF is the first order difference.

```
      :
      :
      ISQ  = 0
      IDIFF = 1
      DO 10 I = 1,NSQ
         ISQ = ISQ + IDIFF
         IDIFF = IDIFF + 2
10    CONTINUE
      :
      :
```

This *incremental* method of computing the squares involves no multiplications and is much faster than the normal method used in the first loop. The table below summarizes the relative execution times for the case where NSQ = 1000:

Compiler	t_{incr}/t_{normal}
Apollo	0.18
Microsoft	0.37
Lahey	0.21
VAX	0.94

Another, more extended, example of incremental computations is borrowed from computer graphics. Assume that the two end points of a line are known and it is required that a line be drawn between the two points. The first approach is to use the equation a straight line, $y = mx + c$, where m is the slope of the line, and c is the y-axis intercept. Next is a subroutine that draws a line by using this equation.

```
      SUBROUTINE LINE(X1,Y1,X2,Y2)
      INTEGER    X1,Y1
      INTEGER    X2,Y2
      INTEGER    I,X,Y
      REAL       M,C,Y

      M  = REAL(Y2-Y1)/REAL(X2-X1)
      C  = Y1 - M*X1
      DO 10 X = X1,X2
         Y  = M*X + C
         CALL SETPIX(X,INT(Y))
   10 CONTINUE
C
      RETURN
      END
```

The routine is very simple. It calls the routine SETPIX, which turns on the pixel at (x,y). Note that x and y are integers. The subroutine LINE first calculates slope m and then the intercept c from the given end points of the required line. It then uses the equation of a straight line to calculate all the pixels that must be set. The routine can only be used to draw lines where x_1 is less than x_2. It is not the fastest method, however, and the standard algorithm employed in computer graphics is Bresenham's line drawing algorithm [21], which will be described briefly. Figure 2.4 shows a line on a video raster. Because of the finite nature of such devices, it is only possible to draw an approximation of a line.

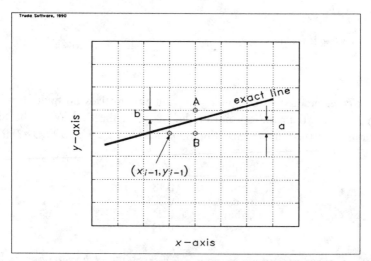

Figure 2.4: Geometry for Bresenham's Algorithm.

If the pixel at (x_{i-1}, y_{i-1}) is set, then either pixel A or pixel B must be illuminated next. Define

$$dy = y2 - y1$$
$$dx = x2 - x1$$

where $(x1, y1)$, and $(x2, y2)$ are the end points of the line. The variables a and b shown in the figure are then:

$$a = y_i + 1 - (dy/dx)$$
$$b = (dy/dx)^*x_i - y_i$$

By comparing a and b, one can decide if A or B must be set. If a is smaller than b, set A, or else set B. It follows from the equations above that

$$(b-a) \quad = 2^*(dy/dx)^*x_i - 2^*y_i - 1$$
$$dx^*(b-a) = 2^*(dy^*x_i - dx^*y_i) - dx$$

Now let $d_i = dx^*(b-a)$, and assume $x1$ is always less than $x2$, so $dx > 0$. If $x1$ is not less than $x2$, one can always swap the end points and force the algorithm to start drawing from the side with the smallest x. With $dx > 0$, if d_i is greater than 0, pixel A must be set, or else pixel B must be set. Thus, d_i can be used to determine which pixel to illuminate. The variable d_i can be calculated iteratively:

$$d_i - d_{i-1} \quad = 2^*(dy^*(x_i-x_{i-1}) - dx^*(y_i-y_{i-1}))$$
$$=> d_i \qquad = d_{i-1} + 2^*(dy^*(x_i-x_{i-1}) - dx^*(y_i-y_{i-1}))$$

Also, (x_i-x_{i-1}) is always 1, and (y_i-y_{i-1}) is either 1 or 0, therefore d_i is

$$d_i = d_{i-1} + 2^*(dy-dx)$$

or

$$d_i = d_{i-1} + 2^*dy + d_{i-1}$$

So d_i can be calculated by adding one of two constants, 2^*dy or $2^*(dy+dy)$, to d_i. These constants need only be calculated once for a particular line. Next is an implementation of Bresenham's algorithm:

```
      SUBROUTINE BRES(X1,Y1,X2,Y2)
      INTEGER   X1,Y1,X2,Y2,DX,DY
      INTEGER   DI,X,Y,AINC,BINC

C Calculate constants for line, and initial di.
      DX   = X2-X1
      DY   = ABS(Y2-Y1)
      AINC = 2*(DY-DX)
      BINC = 2*DY
      DI = 2*DY - DX
      Y  = Y1

C Draw line incrementally.
      DO 10 X = X1,X2
         CALL SETPIX(X,Y)
         IF (DI .GE. 0) THEN
            Y  = Y + 1
            DI = DI + AINC
         ELSE
            DI = DI + BINC
         ENDIF
   10 CONTINUE
      RETURN
      END
```

This routine uses no floating-point arithmetic, but is longer and less flexible than the simple line drawing algorithm, for as it stands, it can only draw lines with slopes between -1 and +1. It is, however, fairly easy to alter the routine to draw lines of arbitrary slope. The routine can give substantial improvement in execution speed on systems where no floating-point support is available. The next table shows measurements for drawing a number of lines, each 150 pixels long, on the IBM PS/2 model 30:

Compiler	t_{Bres}/t_{line}
$MS_{(NO87)}$	0.08
$MS_{(87)}$	0.56

There are two reasons why Bresenham's algorithm is faster. The first is that no floating-point operations are used. The second reason is that it is an incremental algorithm, and it makes optimum use of previous calculations. Without a coprocessor both factors play a role, and Bresenham's algorithm runs about $1/0.08 = 12$ times faster than the routine that uses the equation of a line. With a numeric coprocessor present, eliminating floating-point operations is still a factor in the algorithm's increased efficiency. The incremental nature of Bresenham's algorithm, however, becomes more important, because it cuts down on the total number of calculations, and the algorithm is still almost twice as fast as the other routine. Note, however, that on some systems the time to set a pixel may often be the bottleneck in a line drawing algorithm, and the results on these systems may be disappointing.

The fact that the previous example was drawn from computer graphics is appropriate, for incremental computing is a very important technique in this field. Ivan Sutherland, one of the gurus of computer graphics, and the 1988 recipient of the coveted A.M. Turing award, made the following remarks on incremental computing [22]:

> The man who figured out the basic techniques that made modern graphics possible was David Evans. He had come out of a whole collection of early computing experiences in which incremental computing was used simply because that was all that could be done with the available equipment. He knew that incremental computing was a powerful way to get more results for less work. He suggested to a collection of his students, and to me, that we make use of all the information that we'd computed for one pixel in doing the computations for the adjacent pixel — that we never try to precompute *ab inito*, but rather to compute on the basis of nearby changes. The basic principle of incremental computing is still the mainstay of much high-performance computer graphics today.

In Chapter 9, a more extensive example of incremental computing in computer graphics, namely, polygon filling, is treated in some detail.

2.10 MEMORY-SPEED TRADE-OFF

A fundamental trade-off in computer programming is memory vs speed. Many of the programming techniques discussed so far improve the execution speed of a program at the expense of using more memory, either as larger executable files or as larger data requirements. Sometimes even a small investment in memory can pay off handsomely. For the program 2D in Section 2.3, for example, a 64 x 64 table, which increased the program's memory requirement by a modest 12.5%, improved execution speed by a factor of 2.4 for the Microsoft compiler on a microcomputer. But beware, memory usage is a complicated issue, and larger is not always faster. In fact, the whole of Chapter 5 is devoted to this topic, and throughout the rest of the book frequent references are made to memory management and how it influences efficiency.

One should not confuse larger source files with larger programs. Refer back to Section 2.1. The source code of function ATOI1 is much shorter than that of ATOI2. Small test programs that call the functions are:

```
PROGRAM TEST1                    PROGRAM TEST2
INTEGER ATOI1                    INTEGER ATOI2
K = ATOI1('1')                   K = ATOI2('1')
STOP                             STOP
END                             END

      (b)                             (a)
```

Next are the relative sizes of the executable programs:

Compiler	$Size_{atoi2}/Size_{atoi1}$
Apollo	0.75
Microsoft	0.57

So even though AOI1 appears to be a short, compact routine, it produces larger programs than ATOI2, the apparently larger routine.

2.11 SUMMARY

Several programming strategies were outlined in this chapter, and a central theme is that of a trade-off between two or more factors. One can usually gain speed at the price of more expensive hardware or a better compiler. Efficiency is obtained at the price of reduced flexibility or simplicity. The distinctions between strategies are somewhat synthetic, for a program that uses tables to increase execution speed may be viewed as an example of memory-speed trade-off. It can also be viewed as an example of complexity-speed trade-off, for table look-up makes for a more complex program.

The exact classification of a strategy is beside the point, however. The purpose of this chapter was to give a sense of the various avenues open to a programmer in the quest for an efficient program. If an order-of-magnitude improvement in performance is required, it is unlikely that anything but a better algorithm will suffice. If less improvement is required, and large amounts of memory are available, try to exchange memory for speed. On a system with no floating-point support available, try to eliminate or minimize floating-point calculations by using, for instance, tables or incremental calculations. Faced with a slow program, a programmer should consider all the possibilities.

3

MEASURING EFFICIENCY

Since this book is about computing efficiency, it is appropriate to discuss measuring techniques. The concept of the *profile* of a program was introduced by Knuth [23] in his empirical study of FORTRAN programs. The profile of a program originally referred to a count of the number of times each statement in a program is executed. This concept has proved very useful. One often finds that only a few of the statements in a program account for most of the execution time. Locating these statements can help greatly to improve execution speed.

Profiling has taken on a broader meaning, and profilers available today vary from programs that count the number of times statements are executed, to complex programs that periodically interrupt execution and then note the time and location of the program instruction pointer to determine where execution is. At the end of the program execution, a histogram showing how much time was spent where in the program is produced, and the programmer can study this to improve the program.

3.1 INSTRUMENTATION OF PROGRAMS

As an example of a profiler, consider the Apollo Domain's Histogram Program Count (HPC). It falls into the category of profilers that record the location of the program instruction pointer at regular intervals. To invoke HPC, issue the command:

HPC [*option(s)*] *program*

where *prognam* refers to the name of an executable file, and *option* controls various aspects of HPC. For example, one option (-BRIEF) forces HPC to produce an abbreviated histogram, and another option (-RATE n) sets the number of times per second the program's instruction pointer location is sampled. To illustrate how HPC works, a program called *music* was profiled with HPC. This program called five subroutines: FFT, CSVD, BIT2, EIGEN, and DUMP. Next is the sample run (the "$" in the first line is the Apollo command line prompt):

```
$ HPC -BRIEF -RATE 10000 music

Address  Size      Section
00008040 00002C50  PROCEDURE$
00010000 00004360  DATA$
0000AC90 00000442  DEBUG$

00008980 CSVD              1.4% |*
00008A40 CSVD              2.0% |**
00008D00 CSVD              2.3% |**
00008D40 CSVD              1.2% |*
00008DC0 CSVD              1.7% |*
00008E00 CSVD              1.2% |*
0000A080 CSVD              3.3% |***
0000A0C0 CSVD              2.0% |**
0000A140 CSVD              3.5% |***
0000A180 CSVD              2.9% |**
0000A500 FFT               1.1% |*
0000A540 FFT               1.5% |*
0000A580 FFT               1.1% |*
0000A600 FFT               2.6% |**
0000A640 FFT              17.7% |*****************
0000A680 FFT              17.1% |*****************
0000A6C0 FFT              15.8% |****************
0000A700 FFT               1.6% |*
0000A840 BIT2              1.1% |*
0000AB40 EIGEN             2.0% |**
0000AB80 EIGEN             3.4% |***
         Less than 1%     13.3% |*************
```

The output consists of two parts. The first lists the size and location of the components of the program. The second is the execution histogram, and has four columns that show (a) an address, (b) to what procedure the address belongs, (c) how much time (in %) the program spent in that section, and (d) a graphical representation of that time. Thus, the first line shows that the program spent 1.4% of the time in the 265 bytes from 8980 to 8A40, and this range of addresses is part of routine CSVD. To determine the total time spent in CSVD, one must add up the percentages in the first 10 lines, which gives 21.5%. The same goes for the other routines:

Routine	Relative time (%)
FFT	60.1
CSVD	21.5
Other	13.3
EIGEN	5.4
BIT2	1.6

How does a programmer use this information? It is clear that most time is spent in two routines, namely, FFT and CSVD. To improve program performance, these routines should be the first priority. Also, a significant amount of time (13%) is spent in other sections of the program. This includes execution time for the subroutine DUMP and the operating system overhead (loading and initialization of the program, paging, caching), as well as the overhead of HPC itself.

Similar profiling tools are available on UNIX systems. The easiest to use is the *time* command. To use it, simply issue *time prognam* where *prognam* is the name of an executable file. The operating system will load and execute the program and, when it is done, print some statistics about the program's execution. Here is a sample output:

```
cdu>time order1
Fortran
STOP
                r——————— total time     r——————— Number of page faults.
                v                        v
58.7u 0.0s 1:04 90% 0+0k 0+0io 4041pf+0w
```

This shows that the program took spent 1 min, 4 sec (64 sec) to complete, and that 90% of that time (~ 58 sec) was actually spent executing the program. The program also incurred 4041 page faults (see Section 5.1).

To get more detailed information, a program is compiled with a special compiler switch -**p**. The default output name from the compiler under UNIX is *a.out*, and to profile *a.out*, the UNIX *gprof* program is used:

sdu> gprof a.out

where "sdu>" is the command line prompt. The output from this profiler has several columns, and their significance follows:

Column	Significance
Cumulative seconds:	The running sum of the number of seconds accounted for by this function and those listed above it
Self seconds:	The number of seconds accounted for by this function alone
Calls:	The number of times this function was invoked
Self ms/call:	The average number of milliseconds spent in this function per call
Total ms/call:	The average number of milliseconds spent in this function and its descendants per call
Name:	The name of the function

Here are the abridged results for the program *music* that was profiled with HPC previously:

```
granularity: each sample hit covers 4 byte(s) for 0.01% of 80.29 second
```

% time	cumulative seconds	self seconds	calls	self ms/call	total ms/call	name
30.7	24.61	24.61				mcount (94)
18.8	39.67	15.06	4	3765.00	3942.50	_fft_ [7]
13.8	50.72	11.05	1	11050.00	12792.79	_csvd_ [10]
6.2	55.71	4.99	4162	1.20	1.20	_pars_f [14]
4.7	59.52	3.81	70787	0.05	0.14	_s_wsfe [11]
3.8	62.58	3.06	4165	0.73	3.68	_wrt_F [9]
2.5	64.61	2.03	4165	0.49	0.79	_cvt [16]
			:			
			:			
0.9	76.12	0.71	4	177.50	177.50	_bit2_ [23]
0.8	76.76	0.64	4162	0.15	0.15	_c_sfe [24]
0.7	77.30	0.54				_cabs [25]
0.5	77.67	0.37	4165	0.09	3.76	_w_ed [8]
0.4	78.03	0.36	17854	0.02	0.02	_finite [26]
0.4	78.37	0.34	4162	0.08	0.08	_fmt_bg [27]
			:			
			:			
0.1	79.83	0.08	1	80.00	51986.29	_MAIN_ [3]
0.1	79.89	0.06	1	60.00	60.00	_gendat_ [36]
0.1	79.95	0.06				cont [35]
0.1	80.00	0.05				dsqrt2 [37]
			:			
			:			

It is interesting to note that a large number of routines not referenced in the FORTRAN source are called during execution of the program. Examples include _cabs and _finite. These are low-level routines that the compiler references when compiling the source code. One important routine is the function mcount. This is the function that makes the profile, and accounts for 30.07% of the total execution time.

The routine _MAIN_ corresponds to the main FORTRAN program, and the listing shows that it and its descendants accounted for 5,1986.29 msec, or about 52 sec on this machine. It also shows that the routine _fft_ (which corresponds to FFT in the FORTRAN source) was called four times, and this call and all the routines that it called explicitly or implicitly took 3.94 sec per call. The total time FFT took is therefore 4 x 3.94 = 15.76 sec or 15.76/51.2 ~ 30% of the execution time.

Profilers give results only on a module basis, but one often needs timing information on smaller sections of code. The ideal is a listing that shows how much time was spent executing each line of a program, but the nature of optimizing compilers makes this implausible. Because of the various optimizations (code motion is an obvious example) that these compilers perform, generated code often bears little resemblance to the source code. The best one can do is to get timing information on smaller blocks of code by examining the load map file and finding its correspondence to sections of source code. To get detailed information on a few lines of code, it is necessary to manually perform measurements, and this is the topic of the next section. Nevertheless, profiles are very valuable, for they can help a programmer to rapidly identify time consuming parts of a program without any alterations to the source code.

3.2 MANUAL PROFILING

Computing systems usually provide users, in addition to profilers, with the facility to call the operating system clock. The user can then make calls at selected places in the program and determine the time taken to execute a routine or statement. Indeed, some manufacturers state that this is the preferred way if accurate timing results are needed. To use these system calls effectively, some considerations must be kept in mind, and are the topics of this section.

The subroutine TIMER shown below was written to time FORTRAN program segments on the Apollo Domain system and makes two system calls, TIME_$CLOCK and CAL_$FLOAT_CLOCK. The routine TIME_$CLOCK gets the time from the operating system clock, and CAL_$FLOAT_CLOCK converts the time to a 8-byte real number. Note that the REAL*8 as well as the INTEGER*2 size specifiers are not standard FORTRAN.

```
      SUBROUTINE TIMER(T)
      REAL*8     T
      INTEGER*2  CLOCK(3)
C
      CALL TIME_$CLOCK(CLOCK)
      CALL CAL_$FLOAT_CLOCK (CLOCK,T)
      RETURN
      END
```

The next program uses TIMER to compare the execution time of two subroutines, called ROUTA and ROUTB. The REAL*8 variable that TIMER returns corresponds to a DOUBLE PRECISION variable in the main program.

```
      PROGRAM MANUAL
      DOUBLE PRECISION  T1
      DOUBLE PRECISION  T2

      Y=1.0
      CALL TIMER(T1)
           CALL ROUTA(Y) <———— Time ROUTA
      CALL TIMER(T2)
      TEA=REAL(T2-T1)
      WRITE(*,*)Y
      WRITE(*,*)'Time for ROUTA: ',TEA

      Y=1.0
      CALL TIMER(T1)
           CALL ROUTB(Y) <———— Time ROUTB
      CALL TIMER(T2)
      TEB=REAL(T2-T1)
```

```
WRITE(*,*)Y
WRITE(*,*)'Time for ROUTB: ',TEB
WRITE(*,*)TEA/TEB

STOP
END
```

Here is a sample output:

```
1.1259000E+15
Time for ROUTA: 4.1280388832092290E-03
1.1259000E+15
Time for ROUTB: 1.1199712753295900E-03
3.685843
```

This shows that both routines return the same answer (1.259E+15), but that the routine ROUTA took about 3.7 times longer than ROUTB. The same results were found for other values of Y: both routines produced the same answers, but ROUTA took much longer than ROUTB. This means that ROUTB is preferable because it is faster. Or does it? Below are the two routines:

```
      SUBROUTINE ROUTA(Y)                    SUBROUTINE ROUTB(Y)
      DO 10 I = 1,50                         DO 10 I = 1,50
        Y = Y+Y                                Y = Y+Y
10    CONTINUE                         10    CONTINUE
      RETURN                                 RETURN
      END                                    END

           (a)                                     (b)
```

Surprise! There is no difference (except for their names, of course) between them. What is going on here? The simple approach followed for timing the two routines does not take the overhead the calls to TIMER itself into account, so the measured times are actually the timing overhead plus the actual time for a particular routine. Since the routines are identical, the time difference lies in the timing overhead.

Why is the first timing overhead so much larger than the second? The answer lies in the fact that memory caching (see Section 5.3) takes place on the Apollo. On the very first call to TIMER, it is cached, i.e., brought into the high-speed memory where the CPU will expect to find instructions. Subsequent calls to TIMER will be faster, for the overhead of moving code into cache memory does not exist. So to ensure proper results, one must ensure that TIMER is cached by calling it a few times. Next, measure the overhead, and only then measure computing times. This is shown next:

```
      DOUBLE PRECISION  T1,T2

C Force caching.
      CALL TIMER(T1)
      CALL TIMER(T2)

C Measure timing overhead.
      CALL TIMER(T1)
      CALL TIMER(T2)
      TOV = REAL(T2-T1)

C Measure time for ROUTA.
      Y=1.0
      CALL TIMER(T1)
          CALL ROUTA(Y)
      CALL TIMER(T2)
      TEA=REAL(T2-T1)-TOV
      WRITE(*,*)Y
      WRITE(*,*)'Time for ROUTA: ',TEA

C Measure time for ROUTB.
      Y=1.0
      CALL TIMER(T1)
          CALL ROUTB(Y)
      CALL TIMER(T2)
      TEB=REAL(T2-T1)-TOV
      WRITE(*,*)Y
      WRITE(*,*)'Time for ROUTB: ',TEB
      WRITE(*,*)TEA/TEB

      STOP
      END
```

Here is a sample run:

```
1.1259000E+15
Time for ROUTA: 1.0600090026855470E-03
1.1259000E+15
Time for ROUTB: 1.1320114135742190E-03
0.9563943
```

Now the execution time ratio is about 0.96, 4% short of what it should be, namely, 1. Different runs produced different ratios but all were close to 1.

It is normal for the same program to give varying results, for timings are limited by the resolution of the system clock. On the Apollo this is quite accurate, but on the microcomputer the resolution is about 0.05 sec. The program fragment that one measures should take substantially (say 10 times) longer than this before measurements make sense.

The next example is for the VAX computer. The first step is initialization of the timer routines by calling LIB$INIT_TIMER. This initializes the routines and allocates memory where timing information is stored. To time a particular routine, call the VAX timing routine LIB$SHOW_TIMER before and after the routine. This routine can be called as often as needed in a program. The last step is to free the memory used by the timing routines, and this is done with a call to LIB$FREE_TIMER. After each call to one of the timing functions, another library routine LIB$SIGNAL is used to check for possible errors. The %VAL function referenced in the listing is to force the compiler to pass by value instead of FORTRAN's default pass by reference (see Section 5.6). The example shown is the simplest method of using the VAX system information routines. For more information refer to the *Guide to Programming on VAX/VMS* manual of the VAX [24].

```
      INTEGER*4   TIMER_ADDR,TIMER_DATA,STATUS
      INTEGER*4   LIB$INIT_TIMER,LIB$SHOW_TIMER   ! Timing routines.
      EXTERNAL    LIB$SHOW_TIMER

C Initialize the timer.
      TIMER_DATA = 1
      STATUS = LIB$INIT_TIMER(TIMER_ADDR)
      IF (.NOT.STATUS) CALL LIB$SIGNAL(%VAL(STATUS)) <------ Check for errors.
      .
      :
                                          ┌─┬──── Note "missing" arguments.
C Show timer.                             v v
      STATUS = LIB$SHOW_TIMER(TIMER_ADDR, , ,TIMER_DATA)
      IF (.NOT.STATUS) CALL LIB$SIGNAL(%VAL(STATUS))

      CALL SCALE(I,N)  <──────── Time subroutine: SCALE.

C Show timer again.
      STATUS = LIB$SHOW_TIMER(TIMER_ADDR, , ,TIMER_DATA)
      IF (.NOT.STATUS) CALL LIB$SIGNAL(%VAL(STATUS))
                              └──────────── Pass "STATUS" by value
      .
      :
C Free memory used by timing function.
      STATUS = LIB$FREE_TIMER(TIMER_ADDR)
      IF (.NOT.STATUS) CALL LIB$SIGNAL(%VAL(STATUS))
      STOP
      END
```

The output is shown next, and it has five fields; three are indicated with 1, 2, and 5. The first field shows the total elapsed time, the second field shows the CPU time. The fifth field indicates the number of page faults (see Section 5.1) that has occurred so far.

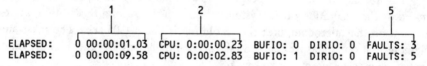

```
          1                  2                              5
          |                  |                              |
ELAPSED:  0 00:00:01.03  CPU: 0:00:00.23  BUFIO: 0  DIRIO: 0  FAULTS: 3
ELAPSED:  0 00:00:09.58  CPU: 0:00:02.83  BUFIO: 1  DIRIO: 0  FAULTS: 5
```

One must subtract the first set of timings from the second to get the elapsed time. For the subroutine SCALE, the total elapsed time is 9.58-1.03 = 8.55 sec. The CPU time is much less: 2.83-0.23 = 2.6 sec. The subroutine SCALE also incurred 5-3 = 2 page faults. Why does the total elapsed time differ so much from the CPU time? The particular installation where this example was executed processes general user programs in a *batch* mode. That is, a number of programs are run as a single task on the computer. Timing starts when the batch is loaded, but the program has to wait its turn before it is executed. The total elapsed time is the "wall clock time," and the CPU time is what a programmer uses to measure execution speed.

3.3 COPING WITH OPTIMIZATION

Say that one wants to measure the time it takes to compute $Y = ASIN(X)$, where $X = 0.1$. Assume that this time is less than the resolution of the system clock, so that the statement must be executed a number of times to get sensible results. The program below is the first attempt:

```
      NC = 10 000
      X = 0.1
      CALL TIMER(T1)   <——————— Force caching
      CALL TIMER(T1)
      DO 10 I = 1,NC
         Y = ASIN(X)
   10 CONTINUE
      CALL TIMER(T2)
      WRITE(*,*)'Time =',(T2-T1)/REAL(NC)
      STOP
      END
```

There are two flaws in the program. The first is that the loop and timing overheads are not accounted for. The second, and more serious, problem is that a compiler that does optimization will figure out that computing $Y=ASIN(X)$ 10,000 times is inefficient, and will eliminate the loop. The code generated by an optimizing compiler is equivalent to:

```
      NC = 10 000
      X  = 0.1
      CALL TIMER(T1)
      CALL TIMER(T2)
         Y = ASIN(X)
      CALL TIMER(T2)
      WRITE(*,*)'Time =',(T2-T1)/REAL(NC)
```

or even to:

```
      CALL TIMER(T1)
      CALL TIMER(T2)
         Y = 0.100167 <——————— Determine value of ASIN(0.1) during compilation
      CALL TIMER(T2)
      WRITE(*,*)'Time =',(T2-T1)/REAL(NC)
```

One can turn off optimization to eliminate this effect, but what if one wants to measure the execution time of a statement with optimization on? In this particular example the execution time of $Y = ASIN(X)$ with or without optimization would be the same, for there is not much to optimize in $Y = ASIN(X)$. With more complicated expressions, turning off optimization will most likely have a major impact on timings.

A general method of dealing with optimization is to place the code one wants to measure in a subroutine and then call the subroutine repeatedly. The subroutine is compiled at full (or any desired level) optimization. To ensure that this method works, one must compile the subroutine separately to hide its inner workings from the main program. In other words, one must prevent global optimization to create the same problem as before. Of course, the overheads of the timing function, the subroutine calls, and the loop must be accounted for.

These overheads can all be combined by creating a dummy subroutine, say DUM(X,Y), that contains nothing but a simple assignment and return statement. The assignment is to force fetching of the parameter X. This subroutine is also compiled separately, for if it is in the same file as the program that calls it, compilers may eliminate it. Applying these ideas to the problem of measuring the execution time of Y=ASIN(0.1) results in the following:

```
SUBROUTINE DUM(X,Y)          SUBROUTINE AS(X,Y)
Y = X                        Y = ASIN(X)
RETURN                       RETURN
END                          END

        (a)                          (b)
```

```
      NC = 10000
      X = 0.1
      CALL TIMER(T1)  <——————— Force caching
      CALL TIMER(T1)
      DO 20 I = 1,NC
         CALL DUM(X,Y) <——————— Call dummy subroutine to measure overhead
   20 CONTINUE
      CALL TIMER(T2)
      TOV = (T2-T1)
      WRITE(*,*)TOV/REAL(NC)  <——————— This is the overhead

      X = 0.1
      CALL TIMER(T1)
      DO 30 I = 1,NC
         CALL AS(X,Y)
   30 CONTINUE
      CALL TIMER(T2)
      WRITE(*,*)'TIME=',(T2-T1-TOV)/REAL(NC)

      STOP
      END
                          (c)
```

It is interesting to see how big the measuring overhead (for Y = ASIN(0.1)) is. On the Apollo it turned out to be about 10%, so that if one did not take it into account, a substantial error would be made. On the IBM model 30 microcomputer with the coprocessor enabled, the overhead was about 15%. With the coprocessor disabled, so that the ASIN function is computed in software instead of hardware, the overhead was negligible compared to the total execution time. There is, of course, not always the need to measure a single statement in such an elaborate way. If the system clock is accurate enough, the execution time for the statement can be measured directly.

3.4 DISCUSSION

Various methods of measuring computing efficiency were discussed in this chapter. The most convenient method is to use profiling programs available at many computing facilities. These programs allow a programmer to quickly determine the most time consuming parts of a program. To get more accurate timings, a programmer can do manual profiling by inserting calls to system timing routines, but it is inconvenient. The program source code has to be altered, and if certain precautions are not followed, improper measurements result.

For example, the UNIX *time* command runs a program and upon completion displays some vital statistics about the program's execution, including the number of page faults. A large number of page faults will point to a program that does not adhere to the locality principle (see Section 5.1), or a program that is input/output bound, and one can apply the techniques of Chapter 7.

In any event, measurements are always important when optimizing programs. A programmer's intuition is often not a good guide when it comes to efficiency, so after each attempt to optimize a program, one should measure to confirm if the program runs faster or not.

4

BASIC OPTIMIZATION

In this chapter some basic optimizations are discussed. Many of the optimizations are usually performed as a matter of course by compilers, so why is it important for a programmer to be concerned with them? Well, it is useful to know how a compiler optimizes a program, for this will enable the programmer to write code in such a manner that the compiler will be able to recognize statements that can be optimized. Also, optimization can lead to some side effects. Knowing what a compiler does when it optimizes code can help in preventing such problems.

4.1 CONSTANT FOLDING

Constant folding refers to the combination (folding into each other) of two or more constants into a single number. Constant folding is done during compilation instead of at run-time. Consider the next two program fragments:

```
PI   = 3.1416                    PARAMETER (PI = 3.1416)
     .                                    .
     :                                    :
TWOPI = 2.0*PI                   TWOPI  = 2.0*PI
PISQR = PI*PI                    PISQR  = PI*PI

     (a)                                 (b)
```

Assume that the variable PI is used as a constant in (a). That is, it is assigned the value 3.1428 and never changed again in the program. The variable TWOPI in (a) is then also a constant since it is the product of two constants, 2.0

and 3.1428. There is no need to perform the multiplication 2.0*PI at run-time; it can instead be done during compilation. This will enhance execution speed. This is an example of constant folding— the two constants 3.1428 and 2.0 are *folded* at compile time. Note that 3.1428 was assigned to a variable PI, and the compiler might not recognize that constant folding is possible, though this is unlikely in this simple example. It is usually better to dec'lare any constants in a PARAMETER statement as in (b). This allows the compiler to recognize and fold constants during compilation. Expressions such as 2.0*PI could be retained to preserve the clarity of the program, while still gaining the benefit of constant folding.

Note that variables that are used as constants in a program but initialized with a DATA statement, are normally treated as "true" variables and are not folded.

4.2   COMMON SUBEXPRESSION ELIMINATION

The expression:

```
A(J+1) = X(J+1+K) + Y(J+1)
```

contains the common subexpression J + 1, which is evaluated three times. This can be reduced to one evaluation by introducing a new variable and rewriting the statement as:

```
N    = J + 1
A(N) = X(N+K) + Y(N)
```

Practically all compilers will be able to recognize the common subexpression in the original statement and do the elimination for the programmer. It is therefore probably best to leave this particular statement as it is. More complex subexpressions might not be recognized, and reordering of terms, or the use of brackets, can be used to assist a compiler to eliminate common subexpressions. Also note that data interference, discussed in Section 4.11, can prevent common subexpression elimination.

4.3   CODE MOTION

When code is moved from one location in a program to another to reduce the number of times the code is evaluated, it is called *code motion*. Code motion usually has its greatest value in DO loops. The expression $1 + N/3$ in (a) below is *loop invariant* (i.e., it does not change inside the loop) and can be moved out of the loop without affecting the result. For the loop in (a), $1 + N/3$ is evaluated 100 times. The code in (b) performs the same function, but $1 + N/3$ is calculated outside the loop. The integer division $N/3$ is now evaluated only once:

```
      DO 10 I = 1,100                    KK = 1+N/3
         K(I) = 1 - I + N/3              DO 10 I = 1,100
 10   CONTINUE                              K(I) = I + KK
                                      10  CONTINUE

         (a)                                   (b)
```

Another example is shown in the following loops:

```
      DO 10 I = 1,M-1                    MM1 = M - 1
         K(I+1-L) = I*I                  LM1 = L - 1
 10   CONTINUE                           DO 10 I = 1,MM1
                                            K(I+LM1) = I*I
                                      10  CONTINUE

         (a)                                   (b)
```

In this example two code motions have taken place. First the repeated calculation of the upper limit of the loop in (a) was moved and is done only once in (b). Second, a part of the calculation of the array index in (a) has been moved out of the loop in (b) and eliminated M-1 subtractions.

Optimizing compilers are quite capable of performing all but the most involved code motions, and in most cases program clarity should be a major consideration. The compiler must of course be able to recognize that code motion can take place, and if expressions are very complicated, a compiler might miss a possible invariant expression. In such cases it is the task of the programmer to manipulate the expressions so that a compiler can recognize the invariant expression or, as an alternative, perform the code motion by hand. Sometimes code motion can result in unpleasant side effects, and this is discussed in Section 4.12.

4.4 STRENGTH REDUCTION

Integer multiplication usually takes longer to perform than integer addition, and is said to be a *stronger* operation than integer addition. In many cases it is possible to replace an expression with an equivalent but less strong one, and this process is aptly called *strength reduction*. The following table lists the relative time taken to perform some of the more common operations on the Apollo DN4000 workstation, IBM PS/2 model 30 microcomputer, and the VAX. Comparisons should be made down the columns, as the table does not compare the running time of the computers against each other. For REAL variables, the measurements were made for the single-precision case. The values in the table should be taken as approximate only.

Operation	Apollo	MS$_{(87)}$	VAX
INTEGER			
subtraction	1	1.2	1
addition	1	1	1
multiplication	21	6.5	1.1
division	34	8.2	1.8
X**N	534		16.2
REAL			
subtraction	80	16	1.4
addition	84	14	1.4
multiplication	90	19	1.4
division	98	23	2.0
FUNCTIONS			
SQRT(X)	98	23	7.6
SIN(X)	136	182	6.3
ATAN(X)	142	130	7.5
EXP(X)	162	186	10.5
TAN(X)	162	376	25.4
LOG(X)	225	195	13.9
ASIN(X)	500	212	21.0
X**Y	760	443	26.0

The table shows that integer subtraction and addition are, not unexpectedly, the fastest operations on the machines. Also, integer multiplication and division are an order of magnitude more expensive than addition on the Apollo, and a factor more expensive on the microcomputer. On the VAX, however, integer multiplication is only about 10% slower than integer addition. According to the table, then, replacing 3*N with N+N+N will increase execution speed on the Apollo, but reduce it on the VAX. In reality N+N+N is compiled as 3*N on the VAX, and 3*N is compiled as N+N+N on the Apollo. In other words, both computers will use the most efficient instructions, and it does not matter if 3*N or N+N+N is given in the source code. This is because optimizing compilers are capable of performing most strength reductions. It is clear that a programmer should not attempt to perform most strength reductions by hand, for it turns out to be largely a waste of time.

For all three computers, division is more expensive than multiplication, but again the ratios vary greatly among the compilers. The most expensive integer operation is X**N, where X is a real number and N an integer. The timings in the table are the average for a large number of N, for execution speed of X**N depends on N. Note that the real exponentiation X**Y (Y is real) takes about 1.6 times longer to perform on the VAX and the Apollo than the integer exponentiation X**N.

The table shows that integer arithmetic is much faster than real arithmetic on the Apollo and the microcomputer. For example, the Apollo takes about 100 times longer to perform real division than integer division. On machines such as these, one can improve the performance of a program dramatically by replacing real with integer arithmetic. A good example of this is Bresenham's line drawing algorithm discussed in Section 2.9. On the VAX, however, the +, -, *, and / operations are almost as fast as their integer counterparts, so one must not assume that algorithms that use integer arithmetic are necessarily faster.

Programming texts that mention efficiency, for instance, frequently advise the programmer to replace division with multiplication where possible, or to set up sine tables instead of repeated calculations, and to avoid the calculation of square roots. Looking at the table, one can see that such statements must be taken with a grain of salt, for they do not apply in general. Depending on the machine, division can be nearly as fast as multiplication, and taking square roots for all intents and purposes just as fast as multiplication. It might be just as fast, if not faster, to recalculate a small number of sines instead of using a table look-up method. The wise programmer should measure execution time before altering code.

4.5 LOOP COMBINATION

The general syntax of a DO loop is:

DO *label*[,] *dovar* = *start*,*stop*[,*inc*]

.
:

label terminal statement.

The square brackets indicate optional items; the loop variable *dovar* is an integer or real variable; *start*, *stop*, and *inc* are integer or real expressions. The default value of *inc* is 1. The range of the DO loop starts at the first statement after the DO statement, and includes the terminal statement of the loop.

A DO loop has several overheads associated with it. The loop variable must be initialized to its starting value. At the end of each iteration a test must be made to determine if the required number of iterations were performed. This is done by testing to see if the expression:

$$MAX(INT(stop - start + int)/inc,0)$$

is zero. If it is, the loop terminates. If it is not, the variable *dovar* is increased by the value *inc*, and the statements in the range of the DO loop are executed once again. Because the control variable of a DO loop must be available outside the range of the loop in FORTRAN, its value must be stored at the completion of each loop. It is often possible to combine one or more loops to save on the loop overhead. This can be done if the range of the loops is the same. This is illustrated by the next example, in which the loops in (a) were combined into the one loop shown in (b):

```
      K = 100                            K = 100
      DO 10 I = 1,K                      DO 10 I = 1,K
        X(I) = REAL(I*I)                   X(I)  = REAL(I*I)
10    CONTINUE                            IY(I) = I
      DO 20 J = 1,K              10     CONTINUE
        IY(J) =  I
20    CONTINUE

         (a)                                   (b)
```

The order in which loops are nested can sometimes be changed to reduce
the loop overhead. The number of initializations of the loop variables of triply
nested loops is shown next:

```
      DO 30 K = 1,25     <─────────── K is initialized once
        DO 20 J = 1,20   <─────────── J is initialized 25  times
          DO 10 I = 1,5  <─────────── I is initialized 500 times
                  .
                  :
10              CONTINUE
20          CONTINUE
30      CONTINUE
```

(a)

With this arrangement, 1 + 25 + 500 = 526 initializations are made; similar calculations can be done for completion tests. In some cases it might be possible to
reorder the loops to reduce the overheads:

```
      DO 30 I = 1,5      <─────────── I is initialized once
        DO 20 J = 1,20   <─────────── J is initialized 5 times
          DO 10 K = 1,25 <─────────── I is initialized 20 times
                  .
                  :
10              CONTINUE
20          CONTINUE
30      CONTINUE
```

(b)

Now the number of initializations of the loop variables totals $1+5+20 =$
26, much less than in the previous case. For multidimensional arrays the order in
which elements are accessed can have a dramatic effect on execution speed. If
the range of the loops above included a statement X(I,J,K) = 4.0 + ..., then the
loop in (a) might very well execute faster than the loop in (b), despite the
smaller loop overheads. Refer to Sections 1.4 and 5.4 for details on this.

4.6 LOOP LINEARIZATION

If a loops runs for a few iterations, it can be replaced by inline code to eliminate
the loop overhead. This is especially true if the calculations done in the loop are
not very time consuming, since the loop overhead then becomes an important

component of the total execution time of the loop. If a loop is replaced with inline code, it is said to be *linearized, unwound,* or *unrolled,* so if (a) below is unwound, the code in (b) results.

```
    DO 10 I = 1,3              X(1) = 2
       X(I) = I + 1           X(2) = 3
 10 CONTINUE                   X(3) = 4
```

        (a)   (b)

The next example shows how to do the loop unwinding to a certain depth [25] . The loop in (a) is unwound to a depth of 4 in (b). The loop increment was modified to count by 4's. For N = 16, for example, the two code fragments process the same number of array elements. For N = 10, two array elements are not accessed by the code in (b).

```
    DO 10  I = 1,N            M = N - MOD(N,4)
       Y(I) = Y(I) + A*X(I)   DO 40  I = 1,M,4
 10 CONTINUE                     Y(I)   =Y(I) + A*X(I)
                                 Y(I+1)=Y(I+1)+A*X(I+1)
                                 Y(I+2)=Y(I+2)+A*X(I+2)
                                 Y(I+3)=Y(I+3)+A*X(I+3)
                            40 CONTINUE
```

        (a)   (b)

In general, MOD(N,K) elements will remain unprocessed with the unrolling method, where K is the unrolling depth and N is the number of iterations the loop must perform. Extra code must be added in these cases to complete the unwinding. The following subroutine SCALE, derived from one by Jack Dongara [26], shows how this is done. The purpose of the routine is to multiply each element of the array SX with the constant SA. Usually a single loop would be used, but here the loop has been unrolled to a depth of five, so MOD($N,5$) elements of SX will not be processed by the unrolled loop. To rectify this, a second loop was added, and this loop will process at most four elements.

```
    SUBROUTINE  SCALE(N,SA,SX)
    REAL     SA
    REAL     SX(*)

C Clean-up loop.
    M = MOD(N,5)
    IF( M .EQ. 0 ) GO TO 20
    DO 10 I = 1,M
       SX(I) = SA*SX(I)
 10 CONTINUE
    IF( N .LT. 5 ) RETURN
```

```
C Unrolled loop.
   20 MP1 = M + 1
      DO 30 I = MP1,N,5
         SX(I)   = SA*SX(I)
         SX(I+1) = SA*SX(I+1)
         SX(I+2) = SA*SX(I+2)
         SX(I+3) = SA*SX(I+3)
         SX(I+4) = SA*SX(I+4)
   30 CONTINUE

      RETURN
      END
```

In some cases substantial gains in speed can be made when unwinding loops. How much is gained depends on what, and how many, operations are performed inside the loop, as well as on the computer that runs the program. The reader is encouraged to perform some measurements to get a feel for how loop unrolling can influence efficiency. The increase in execution speed that results from loop unwinding is especially valuable when applied to short, inner loops of a nested loop structure, for these loops are typically executed many times. The increase in efficiency comes at the price of larger code, and on systems with cache memory it can become counterproductive to unroll a loop too far. This is because cache thrashing (described in Section 5.3) can occur.

4.7 CHARACTER STRINGS

If one must copy one character string or substring to another, it is best not to use a DO loop as in (a) below. Rather, copy the (sub)string with an assignment statement as in (b). The reason the latter is more efficient is that most CPUs have special instructions for copying blocks of data from one location to another. If assignment statements such as (b) are used, the compiler usually generates these fast instructions.

```
      DO 10 I = L,M                    STR1(L:M) = STR2(L:M)
         STR1(I:I) = STR2(I:I)
   10 CONTINUE

         (a)                                  (b)
```

The next table, for example, shows that on all the compilers tested, the DO loop is slower:

Compiler	$t_{assign}/t_{DO\ loop}$
Apollo	0.28
Microsoft	0.02
Lahey	0.04
VAX	0.07

4.8 BOOLEAN EXPRESSION ELMINATION

Compare the next two pieces of code.

```
IF (A.LT.B) THEN              IF (A.LT.B) THEN
        :                             :
        :                             :
ENDIF                         ELSEIF (A.GT.B) THEN
IF (A.GT.B) THEN                      .
        .                             :
        :                     ENDIF
ENDIF

       (a)                            (b)
```

In (a) the variables A and B are always compared twice. In (b), if the condition (A.LT.B) is met, the first block of statements is executed and A and B are compared only once. Thus, in the case of multiple IF-ENDIF blocks, try to combine them into IF-ELSEIF statements to eliminate tests. Also, efficiency can be improved by performing the most likely comparison first, the second most likely second, and so forth.

The precedence of logical operators can be used to early terminate comparisons among logical expressions. In FORTRAN the order in which expressions are evaluated is:

```
        bracketed expressions
        .NOT.
        .AND.
        .OR.
        .EQV. and .NEQV.
```

If a logical expression involves more than one operator, FORTRAN follows a left-to-right evaluation rule. This rule can be used to early terminate a logical expression and hence enhance speed. The most likely and simplest expressions should be placed on the left, and the most complicated and least likely on the right of the expression. Note, however, that function references in a statement may be evaluated in any order according to the FORTRAN standard. Refer to Section 4.12 for the implications of this.

4.9 USE OF BRACKETS

Parentheses can (and should) be used to make the logic of an expression clearer, and also help a compiler optimize code. Brackets can indicate duplicated expressions:

```
A = X*B*Z*Y                  A = B*(X*Y*Z)
C = Z*Y*D*X                  C = D*(X*Y*Z)

      (a)                          (b)
```

A compiler might not be able to recognize the duplicate X*Y*Z in (a), but will almost certainly be able to do so in (b), and can then proceed to optimize by removing the duplicate. Parentheses should also be used to ensure that a compiler recognizes constants in computations. For example:

```
C = 22.1                              C = 22.1
A = 2.0*C*D*E                         A = (2.0*C)*D*E

      (a)                                   (b)
```

The parentheses in (b) can help the compiler to recognize the constant 2.0*C. If these two lines occurred inside a loop, the compiler could then possibly move the computation of 2.0*C outside of the loop, thus eliminating the repeated evaluations of this factor.

4.10 AVOIDING TYPE CONVERSIONS

Converting INTEGER to REAL, or from REAL to INTEGER, etc. (type conversion), takes time, and in some cases as much time as integer addition or subtraction. This is because if a variable appears in an expression where it must be type-converted, not the variable itself, but a copy of the present value of the variable is converted. So the original variable is stored, a copy is made, and the copy is converted and used in further calculations. All this takes time. By simple rearrangement of the expression it might be possible to minimize floating-point conversions. Consider, for example, the next statement:

```
Y = I + L*Y + K + X + NTOT
```

In this expression I, K, and NTOT are integer variables, the rest are real variables. One conversion is made to evaluate L*Y, another to add I to this, another when adding K, and another when adding NTOT. This adds up to a total of four conversions. Rearranging

```
Y = X + L*Y + (I + K + NTOT)
```

gives an equivalent expression but only two conversions are needed.

Unnecessary type conversions can be very costly in ways that are not immediately obvious. Both the statements

```
Y = X**REAL(N)
Y = X**N
```

in which Y and X are floating-point numbers, and N is an integer, perform the same task. The second statement is usually more efficient than the firts. For example, from the table in Section 4.4 it follows that the second statement executes $26/16.2 = 1.6$ times faster than the first on the VAX. The reason for this is that special algorithms exist for integer exponentiation. These algorithms are more efficient than algorithms for real (floating-point) exponentiation, and one such algorithm is discussed in Section 2.6. Some compilers may recognize that the conversion of N from integer to floating-point in the first statement is redundant, and compile the code as $Y = X**N$ and not as $Y = X**REAL(N)$, but not all will. Therefore, a careless type conversion can cost one dearly.

4.11 STATEMENT ORDER AND DATA INTERFERENCE

When variables are used in a sequence of operations or assignments, a simple reordering of the statements may assist an optimizing compiler. For example, in (a) below, the variable X2 does not depend on the variable DT, and the statements can be reordered as in (b). An optimizing compiler can then recognize that the variable B is used in three consecutive statements and keep the variable B in a CPU register, thus enhancing speed.

```
B   = B/(2.0*A)              B = B/(2.0*A)
X1 = B + SQ                  X1 = B + SQ
DT = SQ                      X2 = B - SQ
X2 = B - SQ                  DT = SQ

       (a)                         (b)
```

Now consider the code fragment in (a) below. The variable J may take on the value 1 during program execution, so IA(1) must be fetched from memory twice. The assignment IA(J) = K is said to have *interfered* with the data IA(1). If it is known that J cannot take on the value 1 during program execution, the fragment in (b) will perform the same task as that in (a), but now the value of IA(1) need be fetched only once, which is more efficient.

```
INTEGER IA(100)              INTEGER IA(100)
        .                            .
        :                            :
N      = IA(1)               N      = IA(1)
IA(J) = K                    M      = IA(1)
M      = IA(1)               IA(J) = K

       (a)                         (b)
```

A situation such as this, where memory references prevent optimization of some of the referenced elements, is called *data interference*. Another instance of data interference can occur in the simple loop shown in code fragment (a):

```
      INTEGER IA(100)                        INTEGER IA(100)
        :                                      :
        :                                      :
      I = N + L                              I = N + L
        :                                      :
        :                                      :
      DO 10 J = 1,N                          IT = 2*IA(I)
         IA(J) = 2*IA(I)                     DO 10 J = 1,N
   10 CONTINUE                                  IA(J) = IT
                                          10 CONTINUE

           (a)                                     (b)
```

One's first impulse is to assume that the expression 2*IA(I) is loop invariant, and that an optimizing compiler will generate code that is equivalent to that shown in (b). However, L may be negative, in which case I will be less than N, so the loop in (a) will change IA(I). This implies that 2*IA(I) is not a loop invariant expression as expected, and a compiler cannot generate the more efficient code depicted in (b). If it is known from the algorithm or boundary values of the program that I will always be positive, a programmer should remove loop invariant expressions out of loops such as (a) by hand.

The EQUIVALENCE statement can often lead to data interference that will prohibit optimization. To see how this comes about, consider the next program that declares two arrays IA and IB, and then EQUIVALENCEs them. The program first sets all 10 elements in IB to a value. Next it prints out the values by indexing through IA. Note that in spite of the fact that IA was declared to have only two elements, it is indexed as if it has 10 elements.

```
      INTEGER    IA(2) <——————— IA has 2 elements
      INTEGER    IB(10)
      EQUIVALENCE (IA,IB)
C
      DO 10 I = 1,10
         IB(I) = I
   10 CONTINUE                      ┌——— IA is indexed as if it has 10 elements
C                                   v
      WRITE(*,*)(IA(I),I=1,10)

      STOP
      END
```

This is legal because the two arrays are "equivalent," though some compilers may issue a warning message. In other words, IA might just as well have been declared as

```
      INTEGER   IA(10)
```

In (a) below, two arrays IA and IB are EQUIVALENCEd. A variable K is also EQUIVALENCEd to IB(3) (and therefore also to IA(3)). The variable I can take on a number of values, and if during program execution I becomes 3, the sequence of assignment depicted in (b) will take place. It should be clear that because the variable K was EQUIVALENCEd, it caused data interference with IA(3), and IA(I) must be fetched twice from memory in order for the code to perform as intended. The variable I may never actually become 3, but the compiler has no way of knowing this. It must therefore assume that data interference will take place and generate code accordingly.

```
INTEGER     IA(2)                    INTEGER     IA(2)
INTEGER     IB(10)                   INTEGER     IB(10)
EQUIVALENCE (IB,IA),(IB(3),K)        EQUIVALENCE (IB,IA),(IB(3),K)
IB  = 1                              IB(3) = 1
       .                                    .
       :                                    :
J1  = IA(I)                          J1 = IA(3) ! => J1 = 1
K   = 10                             K  = 10    ! => IB(3)=IA(3)=10
J2  = IA(I)                          J2 = IA(3) ! => J2 = 10

         (a)                                  (b)
```

The primary purpose of the EQUIVALENCE statement is to reduce memory requirements. In the example above, one has saved some space by EQUIVALENCEing the scalar K with the array IB, but this also forced two fetches of IA(I), even in cases where it might not be needed. This is a common problem with the EQUIVALENCE statement; is can often cause the compiler to generate less than the most efficient code. Instances which are particularly troublesome are EQUIVALENCEing of scalars with array elements and EQUIVALENCEing loop indices. This does not imply that the EQUIVALENCE statement should not be used; for example, see Sections 7.5 and 5.5.

4.12 SIDE EFFECTS

Optimization of programs has, like most undertakings, certain pitfalls and hazards of which one should be aware. Because optimizing compilers alter the code during compilation, it is not surprising that some unwanted *side effects* occur. These side effects can be baffling to the unaware. For instance, most compilers do at least some optimizations by default, i.e., they optimize to a degree unless told otherwise. On discovering a bug in a program, the programmer decides to make use of a FORTRAN debugger that is available on the machine.

To make use of the debugger, the program is typically compiled with a special compiler switch set that instructs the compiler to generate code that the debugger will need. This will usually also turn off any optimization. When the programmer steps through the program and examines code and variables, the program produces corrcct rcsults. When the program is again compiled "normally" the bug mysteriously reappears. It is therefore good programming practice to explicitly turn off all optimization during program development and, once it is certain that the program works, systematically increase the level of optimization by using the various compiler switches, carefully checking the results each time. In this way one can establish at what optimization level errors occur.

There are several sources of side effects during optimization of FORTRAN programs, but the most notorious side effects are those associated with functions [27]:

> In general, functions are tricky things if they do anything other than return a value. Unless you are very sure of what you are doing, and the way your function will be called, keep it simple! Regard all values (common and arguments), as 'read-only', and simply write a well-defined final result to the function name. The restrictions are present to allow optimizing compilers to 'deduce' or ignore the value of a function.

Thus

$$A = F(X) + F(X)$$

may be compiled as

$$A = 2*F(X)$$

(some readers of the Standard regard this as unclear, but I believe it is implied) and

$$IF(X.LT.3.OR.F(X).GT.0) \ GOTO \ 1$$

can certainly be compiled as

$$IF(X.LT.3) \ GOTO \ 1$$
$$IF(F(X).GT.0) \ GOTO \ 1$$

or as

$$IF(F(X).GT.0) \ GOTO \ 1$$
$$IF(X.LT.3) \ GOTO \ 1$$

The Standard does not allow you to do anything which would distinguish between these and various cases (and many similar ones).

This is good advice and should be heeded. The author of the article motivates his arguments in terms of what an optimizing compiler might do to code that contains functions. At issue is more than that, for functions that alter their arguments can lead to trouble even in the absence of any optimization. Consider, for example, the next two lines of code:

```
X = 0.87
Y = SIN(X)*COS(X)
```

If the SIN function altered its argument in any way, Y = SIN(X)*COS(X) will not be Y = SIN(0.87)*COS(0.87) as is the obvious intention in this case. Functions that alter their arguments can lead to bugs that are extremely hard to catch, and optimization can further complicate their detection.

Code motion is a possible source of optimization side effects. Consider the next short program. It accepts as input a real number DEN and then scales each element of an array X(I) with the factor NUM/DEN, where NUM is a constant. If the user sets DEN equal to 0.0, one will get a "divide by 0" error, and to guard against this the program checks to see if DEN is zero before performing the division.

```
      REAL    X(4),NUM,DEN
      DATA    X    /1,2,3,4/
      WRITE(*,*)'PLEASE INPUT DENOMINATOR'
      READ(*,*)DEN
C
      NUM = 20.0
      DO 20 I = 1,4
         IF (DEN.NE.0) X(I) = X(I)*(NUM/DEN)
   20 CONTINUE
      WRITE(*,*)(X(I),I=1,4)
      STOP
      END
```

Here is a sample run on a microcomputer running Microsoft FORTRAN, with full optimization:

```
PLEASE INPUT DENOMINATOR
0
run-time error M6103: MATH - floating-point error: divide 0
```

Because of optimization the program did not perform as intended. What happened is that with optimization turned on, the compiler recognized that the factor (NUM/DEN) is loop invariant or constant during execution of the loop, and "hoisted" it out of the loop. The compiler-generated code that is equivalent to:

```
         .
         .
      NUM = 20.0
      R = (NUM/DEN)
      DO 20 I = 1,4
         IF (DEN.NE.0.0)  X(I) = X(I)*R
   20 CONTINUE
         .
         .
```

where R = (NUM/DEN) is probably held in a CPU register. The important thing to notice is that because of the code motion that has occurred, the test to determine if DEN is zero is now performed after the first division by DEN takes place. In other words, the test now becomes useless. To prevent such errors, one has to rewrite the loop, but most compilers will allow a programmer to disable unsafe loop optimizations through the use of compiler switches.

4.13 SUMMARY

This chapter touched on several aspects of program optimization. A central theme is that a programmer should leave basic optimizations to the compiler. It is an interesting experiment to take a piece of FORTRAN code, compile with no optimization, and time its execution speed. Then optimize it by hand, i.e., perform code motions, constant folding, and strength reductions, and again time execution speed. Finally, compile the original code with full optimization, and time execution speed. The results are often surprising (and somewhat humiliating), for the compiler-generated code may execute faster than the hand-optimized code.

More advanced optimizations such as loop unrolling are not usually performed by compilers and should be considered. For the most part, however, a programmer should concentrate on writing clear, straightforward code that will assist the compiler in its task.

5

MEMORY MANAGEMENT

Two aspects of memory management have an influence on programming efficiency. The first depends on the computer's hardware and operating system software. The second is FORTRAN-specific and has to do with the way a FORTRAN compiler stores variables, in particular multidimensional arrays. The simplest memory setup is the case where the computer's CPU is connected directly to the main, or random access, memory. This is shown in Figure 5.1. The program data and instructions are held in RAM, and the CPU fetches data and instructions as needed, loads the proper CPU registers, and executes the instructions. CPU registers are the fastest memory storage elements on a computer, and are immediately available for use by the CPU, so compilers attempt to preserve as many intermediate values in a calculation in registers as possible. After the data is operated upon, it is returned to RAM.

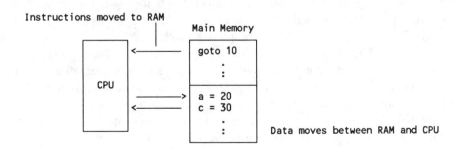

Figure 5.1: Simple Memory Management Scheme for a Computer.

This simple, direct approach is fairly widespread on microcomputers, but is seldom found on high-performance computers, for it has some serious limitations. The first is that the system RAM places constraints on the size of data elements in the program. Consider a program that processes digitized images. Most serious applications need images that are at least 128 x 128 pixels big. On a computer with 640K RAM (common for microcomputers), a single 128 x 128 two-dimensional integer array will use $512^2 \approx 262K \approx 40\%$ of the memory, if the integer word size is 4 bytes.

Common extensions to FORTRAN 77 allow one to specify the word size of integer variables. Assume that each pixel in the image can take on 256 gray levels. Then one can use two-byte integers, i.e., use INTEGER*2 variables. A 256 x 256 INTEGER*2 array can hold the image, but there is still not enough room for a 512 x 512 image, and many algorithms require multiple versions of the same image to be available. An obvious way out of the dilemma is to install more RAM, but this can prove too expensive in practice.

The second problem with the simple memory setup outlined above is that system RAM is often too slow to keep up with the CPU. With data already in the CPU registers, this is no problem, and the CPU can execute at full speed. Any data and instructions that must be loaded from RAM, however, cannot be delivered upon request, and the CPU has to wait a number of CPU clock cycles on each fetch instruction. These idle clock cycles are aptly called *wait states*, and they can degrade a system's performance by as much as 50%. Faster RAM will solve the problem, but high-speed RAM is very expensive.

5.1 VIRTUAL MEMORY AND PAGE FAULTS

The first problem is often solved with an integrated disk storage system that creates what is known as *virtual* main memory. With such a system, called *demand virtual paging memory* (DVPM), the user can define arrays much larger than the computer's physical RAM. The virtual address space is divided into uniform *memory pages*, and the original RAM contains one page (or usually more than one); the rest are on disk storage. When a program references an array element, the system first determines in which memory page the element resides. If the page is in RAM, the program executes normally. If not, the condition is called a *page fault*. In the event of a page fault, the system proceeds to save some of the current RAM contents to disk, and then loads the proper memory page(s) from disk into RAM. This procedure is sometimes referred to as *disk swapping* (Figure 5.2). In this way one can get large amounts of virtual memory, which is in principle limited only by the capacity of the disk storage. While the preceding discussion focused on data, it must be realized that the concept of virtual memory applies to program instructions as well.

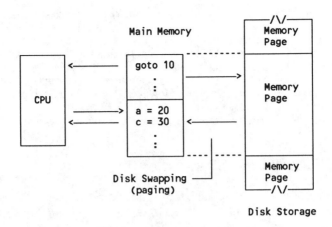

Figure 5.2: Virtual Memory and Disk Swapping.

The basic premise behind such a design is what is known as the *locality principle*. This principle states that memory locations, whether instructions or data, are usually referenced in close proximity by most programs. For example, if the elements of an array are addressed, they are usually close to one another. Also, programs normally do not perform very far jumps, but instead branch to close-by instructions. Therefore, once the proper pages are loaded, little disk swapping occurs.

DVPM is implemented with a combination of hardware and software, and page sizes depend on various factors, 4K being not uncommon. The Motorola 68030 CPU, used on popular engineering workstations such as the Apollo and the Sun, supports, for instance, page sizes from 256 bytes to 32K, while the Intel 80386 supports 4K page sizes. DVPM works remarkably well in practice *if* programs do not violate the underlying assumption, namely, the locality principle. A program that does not adhere to this principle will produce a large number of page faults, and this will quite often be the major culprit in a slow program. In practical terms, in order to reduce page faults, try to write programs that adhere to the locality principle. Thus:

- Code should not jump all over the place, and
- Address memory as sequentially as possible.

Note that virtual memory has particular importance in FORTRAN. Many computer languages allow dynamic memory allocation. This means a block of memory can be allocated as needed during program execution, and when the block is no longer needed, the block can be deallocated, or returned to the operating system. Unfortunately, standard FORTRAN does not have this capability, so that [28]:

Fortran's static memory allocation makes it necessary to always declare arrays to be big enough to handle the largest expected data set, which is inefficient and poses a real problem for computers with limited memory like IBM-PCs. Virtual memory is a distinct advantage for Fortran programming because arrays can be huge without running out of virtual memory; the operating system automatically takes care of dynamic memory allocation. However, the memory really isn't limitless, even if it looks that way, and a failure to understand the basic mechanics of virtual memory can lead to serious inefficiencies.

5.2   OVERLAY LINKERS

A somewhat different, but related, topic is the so-called *overlay linkers* found on microcomputers. These programs create special versions of the executable files that enable execution of programs much larger than the microcomputer's RAM. During linking, the overlay linker will create a program that has a resident part and several *overlays*. Overlays are restricted to modules (functions or subroutines) and data are not overlaid. When the program is executed, the resident part is read from the executable file, loaded, and executed. Whenever an overlaid module is referenced, the program reads the overlay module into memory to become the new resident part. True disk swapping does not occur, for all the executable statements are already on disk.

To improve execution speed, one would want to reduce disk access as much as possible, so a programmer should avoid using overlays. The user can usually specify which modules are to be overlaid, so when overlays are used, modules that must be overlaid must be carefully chosen. Consult the particular overlay linker's user manual for specific information.

5.3   CACHE MEMORY

The simple memory management scheme outlined in the introduction has a second problem, that of a CPU too fast for RAM. The solution is a small amount of memory that can keep pace with the CPU. It is used as a buffer or *cache memory* between the CPU and main memory. Data that is most often referenced is then kept in this memory. This reduces the CPU wait states and improves efficiency. The larger the cache memory, the more effective the scheme will be, but the more expensive the system will become. Special hardware attempts to ensure that the most frequently used data is in the cache memory, but it does not always succeed. If requested data is in the cache, it is called a cache *hit*, and if it is not (what else?) a cache *miss*. The cache hit ratio is an important indication of the effectiveness of a cache system. The hit ratio depends on many factors, including cache type, size of the cache memory, and the program that is executing on the computer (Figure 5.3).

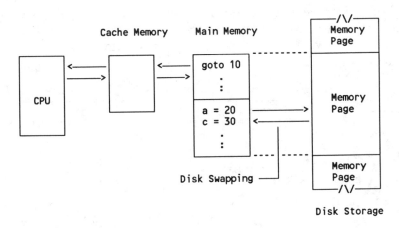

Figure 5.3: Cache Memory.

Caching is not limited to data and applies to program instructions as well. Many modern processors found in engineering workstations have data as well as instruction caches incorporated on the CPU chip. The typical size for these *internal* caches is 256 bytes, and they work in tandem with larger external caches. Even a small amount of cache (say 32KB) can provide dramatic improvements in system performance; it will often ensure hit rates well above 85% and improve system performance by as much as 40-50%. Because of this, memory caches are becoming fairly widespread in high-end microcomputer systems.

Cache memory is prone to a phenomenon known as *thrashing*, which occurs, for example, if all the elements of an array are continually referenced but only part of the array fits into the cache. The cache is then repeatedly reloaded, and more time is spent moving data into the cache and then to the CPU than direct transfers from RAM would take. The same holds true for instructions. Figure 5.4 shows a loop that fits completely into the instruction cache.

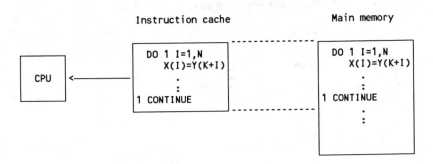

Figure 5.4: Loop Fits in Instruction Cache, and No Thrashing Occurs.

When the program executes, the instructions that make up the loop will be loaded once from the main memory into the instruction cache, and it will execute efficiently. Figure 5.5 shows a loop that is too large to fit into the instruction cache.

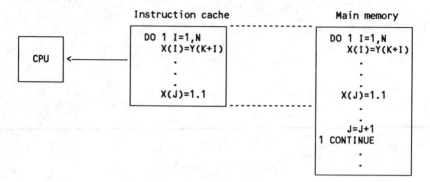

Figure 5.5: Loop Overflows Instruction Cache, and Thrashing Occurs.

Because this longer loop does not fit into the cache, the first part of the instructions is loaded into the cache and executed. Then the cache is flushed, and the second part of the instructions is loaded and executed, and so on. This is quite inefficient. It is therefore important that loops (especially inner loops) be as tight as possible so they can fit into the instruction cache.

5.4 REFERENCING MEMORY

Consider a two-dimensional array X, declared with DIMENSION X(2,3). This array has three columns, and each column has two rows. In FORTRAN the array X is stored as indicated in Figure 5.6, i.e., column after column. Since the columns of X are stored sequentially, this is called a *column-major* order, also referred to as FORTRAN indexing, or the FORTRAN index.

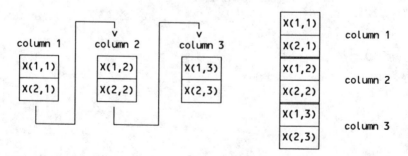

Figure 5.6: Column after Column Storage of a 2 x 3 Array in FORTRAN.

Not all programming languages follow this convention; PASCAL and the C programming language store arrays row after row, and therefore follow a *row-major* ordering. Some compilers offer the facility to specify whether column- or row-major ordering must be followed. This is important in systems that support mixed-language programs, where a FORTRAN program can, for instance, call a compiled C subroutine or vice versa. It stands to reason that the same conventions must be followed in such cases.

Returning to the array X, it is readily seen that the address of an element X(I,J) is given by:

```
Element_address = Array_Base_Address + I + (J-1)*Number_of_rows
```

where Array_Base_Address is some starting address that the compiler/linker assigns to the first element of X. For the rest of the discussion here Array_Base_Address will be taken as zero, but it does not alter the validity of the statements made. Note that the leftmost index of a multidimensional array varies the fastest in FORTRAN, then the next to leftmost index, and so on.

One method of referencing the elements in the array is shown in (a) below, and the order in which they will be accessed in memory is shown in (b). This method forces the compiler to generate code that references each element of the array by calculating the address of the first element of each column, then calculates the address of the second element in each of the three columns.

```
        REAL X(2,3)              Address of X(1,1) is 1+(1-1)*2 = 1
        DO 20 I=1,2                "     "  X(1,2) is 1+(2-1)*2 = 3
           DO 10 J=1,3             "     "  X(1,3) is 1+(3-1)*2 = 5
              X(I,J)=1.0           "     "  X(2,1) is 2+(1-1)*2 = 2
10         CONTINUE               "     "  X(2,2) is 2+(2-1)*2 = 4
20      CONTINUE                  "     "  X(2,3) is 2+(3-1)*2 = 6

           (a)                              (b)
```

An alternative way to access array elements is to switch the order in which the elements are addressed. This is shown next. Now the elements are referenced in the order in which they are stored in memory.

```
        REAL X(2,3)              Address of X(1,1) is 1
        DO 20 J = 1,3              "     "  X(2,1) is 2
           DO 10 I = 1,2           "     "  X(1,2) is 3
              X(I,J) = 1.0         "     "  X(2,2) is 4
10         CONTINUE               "     "  X(1,3) is 5
20      CONTINUE                  "     "  X(2,3) is 6

           (a)                              (b)
```

The computer can address all the elements just by incrementing a counter until all the elements have been indexed. Since the addresses of the elements are now found by simply incrementing a counter, it is more efficient than the first method, and one should, where possible, try to vary the leftmost subscript of multidimensional arrays the most rapidly.

The discussion so far focused on the cost of memory address calculations. On machines with virtual memory management (see Section 5.1) some elements of large arrays might actually exist on disk, so that page faults occur, which will then dominate execution time. A general principle is therefore to *address memory as sequentially as possible*. This will possibly (a) reduce the number of address calculations and (b) on systems with virtual memory, reduce the number of page faults.

5.5 ARRAY INITIALIZATION

Loop overhead can be minimized in the initialization of multidimensional arrays. Since FORTRAN stores arrays sequentially in memory, one can use one loop to initialize all the dimensions. Consider the next initialization of a three-dimensional array X. Here all the elements are set to the variable T.

```
      REAL   X(5,20,25)                           REAL       X(5,20,25)
         .                                        REAL       Y(2500)
         :                                        EQUIVALENCE (X,Y)
      DO 30 I = 1,5                                  .
        DO 20 J = 1,20                               :
          DO 10 K = 1,25                          DO 10 I = 1,2500
            X(I,J,K) = T                             Y (I) = T
10          CONTINUE                        10    CONTINUE
20        CONTINUE
30    CONTINUE

           (a)                                          (b)
```

In the computer's memory the array is stored as 5 x 20 x 25 = 2500 consecutive data elements. This fact can be exploited to write the loops as shown in (b). Note that since X and Y are EQUIVALENCEd they share the same memory, and initializing Y also initializes X. Also, no extra memory is used in defining Y, since the compiler does not allocate extra memory for EQUIVALENCEd variables. Making use of this technique involves one extra declaration but saves the overhead of three loops.

5.6 SUBROUTINES AND PARAMETERS

Subroutines (functions are also considred subroutines for the sake of discussion in this section) and functions are used to remove blocks of statements from one program to another (sub)program. Subroutines have a number of advantages, such as saving program space and improving readability of the program, thus making it easier to modify and debug. It is considered good programming practice to *make sure every module hides something* [29]. It also enables separate compilation so that one can build a library of compiled functions for later use by programs. From an efficiency standpoint, however, some disadvantages exist.

The first is that each subroutine call involves an overhead that direct inline code does not have. FORTRAN is somewhat more efficient than some other languages in this respect. This is because it passes subroutine parameters by *reference* instead of by *value*. Passing a parameter by reference means that the address of the parameter is passed to the called subroutine, and passing by value means that a copy of the parameter is made, and then the copy is passed via a stack to the subroutine. To make the copy takes time, making passing by value slower. Also, in a language such as C, a routine can have a variable number of arguments passed to a subroutine, so the called routine must each time figure out how many arguments were passed on that call. This also slows things down, but FORTRAN does not have this overhead.

While FORTRAN passes variables by reference, some compilers provide language extensions to facilitate passing by value; for instance, the %VAL function on the VAX compiler can be used to pass a variable by value. One can also force passing by value in standard FORTRAN. It occurs when an actual argument to the called subroutine is enclosed in parentheses, or when the argument is a legal expression other than a simple variable name. For example, after the call to SWAP in (a) below, N = 2 and M = 1, i.e., their values were swapped. In (b), the actual arguments N and M are enclosed by parentheses, and call by value occurs. In other words, the subroutine SWAP will receive the addresses of copies of N and M, and swap the copies. In the main program their values will remain unaltered.

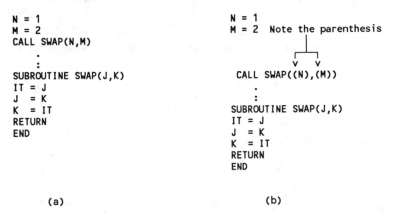

```
N = 1
M = 2
CALL SWAP(N,M)
   .
   :
SUBROUTINE SWAP(J,K)
IT = J
J  = K
K  = IT
RETURN
END


        (a)
```

```
N = 1
M = 2  Note the parenthesis

CALL SWAP((N),(M))
   .
   :
SUBROUTINE SWAP(J,K)
IT = J
J  = K
K  = IT
RETURN
END


        (b)
```

Passing by value therefore protects the variables in the calling program from modification by a subroutine, and is often the preferred method in other languages. It is slower and, while available, not really "typical" FORTRAN.

The second problem with subroutines is exactly because they "hide something," and optimizing compilers cannot perform global program optimizations. For instance, if a piece of code is moved from the main program to a subroutine, a compiler might not be able to perform some of the optimizations. The individual modules will still be optimized, though. If the main program and the subroutine are compiled separately, which is often the case, even fewer intramodular optimizations are possible.

The way in which variables are passed between subprograms influences speed. Passing variables among subprograms is the fastest on most computers when passed in a COMMON block. COMMON blocks introduce global variables, which should usually be kept to a minimum for the sake of clear, modular programs. On the other hand, because a COMMON block is referenced in both subprograms, some addresses are calculated during compilation. Passing variables as parameters involves a parameter list, which is an overhead that passing via COMMON does not have.

5.7 DECLARING VARIABLES

If a program has arrays of different lengths, one should consider increasing the shorter ones so that they all have the same length. This would enable an optimizing compiler to use indices calculated for one array for indexing another array. Common sense should prevail, however, and it makes no sense to enlarge smaller arrays so much that too much memory is wasted. On the other hand, if one can add an element or two to make lengths equal, it should be considered.

The order in which variables are declared in COMMON blocks may influence the efficiency. Metcalf [30] argues convincingly that the best ordering on the IBM VS compilers are scalars, followed by small arrays, followed by large arrays; his reasoning can be extended to other compilers as well. Therefore,

```
INTEGER           N,L,K
REAL              A,B
REAL              DTA(10),RARR(100)
DOUBLE PRECISION  DARR(10)
COMPLEX           CARR(10)

COMMON    /ALL/   N,L,K,A,B,DTA,RARR,DARR,CARR
```

is preferable to

```
INTEGER           N,L,K
REAL              A,B
REAL              DTA(10),RARR(100)
DOUBLE PRECISION  DARR(10)
COMPLEX           CARR(10)

COMMON    /ALL/   RARR,CARR,K,B,DTA,A,DARR,L,N
```

It is also good to group variables in a COMMON block by their logical use in a program, for it may lead to more efficient address calculations. In (a) below, the variables A and B are stored with 511 real variables between them, but note that in the program they are logically "close" to each other. In (b) they are stored next to each other. A compiler can find the address of one of the variables by simply incrementing or decrementing the address of the other, which is very efficient.

```
REAL   BLOCK(511)              REAL   BLOCK(511)
COMMON /DTA/ A,BLOCK,B         COMMON /DTA/ A,B,BLOCK
        .                              .
        :                              :
A = B+2*A                      A = B+2*A
        .                              .
        :                              :
       (a)                            (b)
```

5.8 MEMORY SEGMENTATION AND MEMORY MODELS

Some processors, such as the 8086 family of CPUs used in the IBM PC, divide the memory address space into *memory segments*. This is the result of the limited word size (16 bits) of the CPU registers, which can take on $2^{16} = 65,536$ (64K) different values. Thus, if a CPU register is used as an index register, it can address 64K memory locations. To address more memory locations, two registers are used. One is used as a base and the other holds an offset address from the base. Two 16-bit CPU registers can in principle address $2^{16} \times 2^{16} = 4.2 \times 10^9$ memory locations. There is more to memory segmentation than this simple explanation, but this will suffice for the purposes of this book.

If a program is small enough, a compiler can generate code that fits completely into a segment of 64KB of memory. Depending on the size and data requirements, a program might need a data segment as well as a code segment, a data segment and multiple code segments, or even multiple data and multiple code segments. These various combinations are called memory *models*, and some of the common models are summarized as follows:

Model	Description
Medium	Total program data restricted to 64K, but program code can exceed 64K. The compiler generates multiple code segments as needed.
Large	Program code and data can both exceed 64K, but formal array arguments are not allowed to exceed 64K. The compiler again generates multiple code and data segments as needed.
Huge	Same as large model, but 64K limit on formal array arguments lifted.

If multiple segments are used, a single register is no longer used to address the memory, and performance is degraded. This is because the process of managing the segment registers introduces an overhead which takes time. Also,

CPU registers used for managing segments are not available for the compiler to use in optimizations. A third reason is that some CPU instructions for efficient data manipulation do not always work properly across segments, and the compiler has to generate alternative, less efficient code. For example, the 8086 CPU REP MOVSW instruction can be used to efficiently copy or move blocks of memory from one location to another. Next is a short program that copies the contents of an array MATA to an array MATB. The default INTEGER word size for Microsoft FORTRAN is 4 bytes, so that the program in effect copies 16,000 bytes from one location to another.

```
      INTEGER     MATA(4 000 )
      INTEGER     MATB(4 000 )
      DO 10   J = 1,4 000
          MATB(J) = MATA(J)
   10 CONTINUE
      STOP
      END
```

The Microsoft FORTRAN compiler has a /Fa switch that generates an assembly language listing if a program is compiled with the switch set. Next is an edited version of the assembly listing for the program above, which was compiled with full optimization. Note that the assembly listing has no loop; the compiler is smart enough to realize that it can use a REP MOVSW instruction to copy the data.

```
        .
        :
  mov  WORD PTR $S16_J,1      ; DO loop variable J=1
  mov  WORD PTR $S16_J+2,0

  mov  WORD PTR [bp-4],OFFSET DGROUP:$S_MATB
  mov  bx,WORD PTR [bp-4]
  push ds
  pop  es
  mov  di,bx                  ; es:di points to MATB

  mov  WORD PTR [bp-6],OFFSET DGROUP:$_MATA
  mov  ax,WORD PTR [bp-6]
  mov  si,ax                  ; ds:si points to MATA

  mov  cx,8000                ; Number of 2-bytes to copy
  rep  movsw                  ; copy 16,000 bytes <———————— Efficient Copy

  add  WORD PTR $S16_J,4000   ; J at end of loop
  adc  WORD PTR $S16_J+2,0    ; J = 1 + 4000
        .
        :
```

The listing has five parts, each separated with a blank line. The first part initializes the DO loop variable J ($S16_J in the assembly listing) by setting it to 1. The next part loads the destination (MATB) address into the ES:DI register pair, and the third part loads the DS:SI registers with the source (MATA) address. The fourth part loads the CX register with the number of 2-bytes (8000 in this case) to copy. With the required registers properly loaded, 16,000 bytes are copied with the REP MOVSW instruction. In the last part, the DO loop variable J is set to its required value at exit for a DO loop, namely 4001, in this case.

Shown in Figure 5.7(a) is a similar program, but now 10,000 integers are copied, which is equivalent to 4 x 10,000 = 40,000 bytes. The 40,000-byte arrays MATA and MATB are too large to both fit into a single 64K segment, so two segments are needed. To ensure this, the program was compiled with the /Gt Microsoft FORTRAN compiler switch, which forces any data element greater than 255 bytes into a separate segment. This is depicted in Figure 5.7(b).

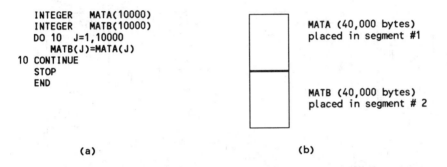

```
      INTEGER   MATA(10000)
      INTEGER   MATB(10000)
      DO 10   J=1,10000
         MATB(J)=MATA(J)
10 CONTINUE
      STOP
      END


          (a)
```

MATA (40,000 bytes)
placed in segment #1

MATB (40,000 bytes)
placed in segment # 2

(b)

Figure 5.7: Two Segments are Generated When the /Gt Switch is Used.

The **/Fa** compiler switch was again used to produce an assembly language listing of the program :

```
      ⋮
      mov   WORD PTR $S16_J,1      ; DO loop variable J = 1
      mov   WORD PTR $S16_J+2,0
      mov   si,OFFSET $S15_MATB+4  ; si points to start of MATB
      mov   di,OFFSET $S14_MATA+4  ; di points to start of MATA
      mov   cx,10000               ; Number of iterations
      add   WORD PTR $S16_J,10000  ; J at end of DO loop
      adc   WORD PTR $S16_J+2,0

$L20001:                           ; Top of loop        <──────┐
      mov   bx,di                  ; Load segment registers      │
      mov   es,$T20002             ; for source (MATA)           │
      mov   ax,WORD PTR es:[bx-4]  ; Move element from MATA      │
      mov   dx,WORD PTR es:[bx-2]  ; to ax and dx                │
      mov   bx,si                  ; Load segment registers      │
      mov   es,$T20003             ; for destination (MATB)   loop│
      mov   WORD PTR es:[bx-4],ax  ; Move contents of ax and dx  │
      mov   WORD PTR es:[bx-2],dx  ; to MATB                     │
      add   si,4                   ; Next element in MATB        │
      add   di,4                   ; Next element in MATA        │
      loop  $L20001                ; Decrement CX, and repeat    │
                                   ; loop if CX not 0 ──────────┘
      ⋮
```

Here the compiler did not use the REP MOVSW instruction. This is because the data is copied across segments, and REP MOVSW is not reliable in such cases. A true loop was thus generated, and the comments in the listing indicate the various parts of the loop. Because the 8086 CPU does not support memory-to-memory data transfers, each element must be copied from memory to the CPU registers, and then from the CPU registers to memory. Note that since each array element is 4 bytes wide, and the 8086 CPU registers are only two bytes (16 bits) wide, two data transfers are needed for each element. The copy process is illustrated in Figure 5.8.

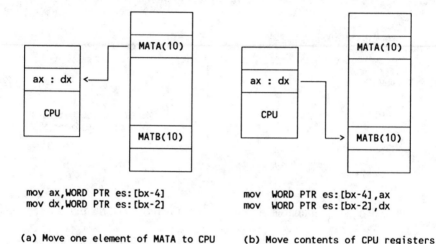

```
mov ax,WORD PTR es:[bx-4]                    mov  WORD PTR es:[bx-4],ax
mov dx,WORD PTR es:[bx-2]                    mov  WORD PTR es:[bx-2],dx
```

(a) Move one element of MATA to CPU   (b) Move contents of CPU registers
    registers ax and dx.   ax and dx to MATB.

Figure 5.8: Copying MATA(10) to MATB(10).

In (a), two bytes of MATA(10) are copied to the AX CPU register, then the next two bytes of the element to the DX CPU register. In (b), the contents of the AX register, and then the contents of the DX register are moved to MATB(10). Also, to move the element, two sets of segment registers had to be loaded (see the assembly listing). It should come as no surprise, then, that the second program takes much longer (about 4.5 times) to copy the array.

5.9 DISCUSSION

It should be clear that memory management is a complex issue. It has an important influence on execution speed as well as on programming strategies. There are large differences in memory management schemes among computers, but despite these differences, one can draw two conclusions. The first is that a programmer should attempt to address memory as sequentially as possible. This implies that multidimensional arrays must be indexed according to the

FORTRAN index, i.e, varying the leftmost index the fastest. This is especially true on systems with virtual memory management and for programs that use large data arrays. The second observation is that the size of a program module has an influence on the run-time efficiency of the program. On MS-DOS-based microcomputers with their segmented memory, for example, programs that stay under a 64K limit for code and/or data will execute faster than larger programs. The influence of program size on execution speed also is not limited to micro-computers. On the IBM VS FORTRAN compiler, for example, the threshold is 8192 bytes, and programs that compile to code less than this execute faster.

6

PROGRAM GENERATION

As algorithms become more powerful, one usually finds that they also become more complex. Often this increased complexity is in sequencing and decision making within the algorithm at run-time. In the process of refining the implementation of an algorithm, one might, for instance, include loops and program sections to handle special cases. While this may speed things up, it also increases the overhead by testing for these special cases at run-time. Morris [31] introduced the program generation concept to reduce this often time consuming loop and program flow control, and much of this chapter was taken (rather shamelessly!) from his work.

The basic idea behind program generation is simple: in some applications the same subroutine is used over and over, and the only difference between runs is the data. By creating a tailor-made program that minimizes or completely eliminates the number of *data-independent* calculations, one can improve efficiency. An obvious drawback is that if the number of data points changes, then a new program must be coded. In the program generation technique, however, another computer program is used to generate the specialized program needed for a particular application, so that once a generator program exists, little effort is required. Because the custom program is created with another computer program, program generation is also called the *autogen method*, and several variations exist. They are:

- Inline code
- Threaded code
- Knotted code

The different methods are best explained in terms of a concrete example, and the computation of the autocorrelation of a sequence of numbers is used for this purpose. Two complete examples of program generation are also given, one an inline FFT generator, and the other a threaded code FFT program.

6.1 INLINE CODE

The digital autocorrelation $r(k)$ of an N-point sequence of numbers $x(n)$ is given by:

$$r(k) = \sum_{n=1}^{N} x(n)x(n+k), \quad k = 0, 1, \ldots$$

Conceptually, the autocorrelation is calculated by taking the original sequence, and then multiplying it with a shifted version of itself, using only data points that overlap. If, for example, the data sequence is 1, 2, ..., 8, then the $r(1)$ is calculated as

```
1  2   3    4    5    6    7    8       <─────────  Original sequence
   1   2    3    4    5    6    7    8   <─────────  Shifted sequence
   ─────────────────────────────────
   2  +6  +12  +20  +30  +42  +56   = 168
   ─────────────────────────────────
```

which needs six additions and seven multiplications to compute.

Autocorrelation finds application in number of digital signal-processing problems, including *linear prediction* (LP) which is widely used in speech analysis and synthesis. It is often the case in these applications that only a few points of the autocorrelation sequence are needed. For example, with the length of $x = 1024$, only the first 128 points of $r(k)$ may be required. Computing the autocorrelation using the equation above then becomes inefficient. An algorithm that almost halves the number of multiplications if the required number of autocorrelation points are much fewer than the length of the data sequence, is the Pfeifer-Blankinship [32], [33] autocorrelation algorithm:

$$r(k) = \sum_{j=0}^{q-1} \sum_{i=1}^{k} x(2jk+i+k)[x(2jk+i)+x(2jk+i+2k)]$$

where $q = \lceil N/2k \rceil$, $x(n)=0$ for $n > N$, and $1 \leq k \leq N/2$. To compute $r(1)$ for the previous 8-point sequence with the Pfeifer-Blankinship algorithm one would use:

$$
\begin{aligned}
r(1) = \quad & x(2)(x(1)+x(3)) \\
+ \quad & x(4)(x(3)+x(5)) \\
+ \quad & x(6)(x(5)+x(7)) \\
+ \quad & x(8)^*x(7)
\end{aligned}
$$

$$=> \; r(1) = \quad 2(1+3) + 4(3+5) + 6(5+7) + 7*8$$
$$= \quad 168$$

This computation needs six additions and four multiplications, which is about half of the number of multiplications needed for the first method. Next is an implementation of the Pfeifer-Blankinship algorithm:

```
        SUBROUTINE ACORR (X,N,MP1,R)
        REAL      R(*)
        REAL      X(*)
        INTEGER   N,MP1
C
        R(1) = 0.0
        DO 10 I = 1,N
           R(1) = R(1) + X(I)*X(I)
10      CONTINUE
C
        DO 40 JJ = 2,MP1
           NDEL  = JJ-1
           R(JJ) = 0.0
           NQ    = N/(2*NDEL)
           NN    = 2*NDEL*NQ
           IF (NN .NE. N) NQ = NQ+1
           DO 30 JK = 1,NQ
              JL  = JK - 1
              NB1 = NDEL*(2*JL+1)
              NB2 = NDEL*(2*JL)
              NB3 = NDEL*(2*JL+2)
              DO 20 I = 1,NDEL
                 N1 = NB1 + I
                 N2 = NB2 + I
                 N3 = NB3 + I
                 IF (N2 .GE. N) GOTO 30
                 IF (N3 .LE. N) TERM = X(N1)*(X(N2)+X(N3))
                 IF (N1 .GT. N) GOTO 30
                 IF (N3. GT. N) TERM = X(N1)*X(N2)
                 R(JJ) = R(JJ) + TERM
20            CONTINUE
30         CONTINUE
40      CONTINUE

        RETURN
        END
```

The array X holds the input sequence of length N, and R is the computed auto-correlation. The variable MP1 is the number of points of the autocorrelation that must be calculated. The subroutine ACORR uses the default FORTRAN lower dimension bound of 1, so indexing in the subroutine differs slightly from the definition of the autocorrelation. However, FORTRAN does allow one to specify the lower dimension bound of arrays. A program that calls ACORR can therefore use the same indexing as in the definition of the autocorrelation, simply by declaring R with a lower dimension bound of 0. The following example should make this clear:

```
        REAL    X(8)
        REAL    R(0:15)  <——— Lower dimension bound of R is 0

        N   = 8
        MP1 = 3
        DO 10 I = 1,N
            X(I) = REAL(I)
   10   CONTINUE

        CALL ACORR (X,N,MP1,R)
        WRITE(*,'(20F8.3)')(R(I),I=0,4)
        STOP
        END
```

The input sequence is 1, 2, ..., 8, and ACORR is called with MP1 = 3, so after
the call to ACORR, R will contain the first three terms of the autocorrelation of
the input, namely, $R(0) = 204$, $R(1) = 168$, and $R(2) = 133$.

While this algorithm reduces the number of multiplications, it does not
necessarily reduce execution speed, for the increased complexity in terms of
loops and execution control at run-time can offset any gains made. In a typical
application of autocorrelation, namely, speech analysis, a routine that computes
the autocorrelation will be called many times. While the data changes between
calls, the number of data points, as well as the number of points of the autocorrelation sequence needed, stays the same. So each time ACORR is called, all
the jumps and array indices must be calculated over again.

An alternative is to create a specialized subroutine that contains all the
data-independent calculations, and the resulting program is a simple *inline*
expansion of the Pfeifer-Blankinship algorithm. The inline code for computing
the first term of the autocorrelation for an 8-point data sequence is shown next:

```
        REAL        X(8)
        CALL GET(X) <——— Get data sequence

        R = 0.0
        R = R + X(2)*(X(1) + X(3))
        R = R + X(4)*(X(3) + X(5))
        R = R + X(6)*(X(5) + X(7))
        R = R + X(8)*X(7)
   C
        WRITE(*,*)'R(1) = ',R
        STOP
        END
```

This code has no jumps, loops, or other control structures, and at run-time
each statement operates only on the data, and the program is very efficient.
Unfortunately, inline code has a serious down side. For all but the simplest
algorithms and short data sequences, inline programs become very large exactly
because they are inline — all statements are expanded. The memory-speed
trade-off is also often nonlinear. That is, with small data sequences the speed

gained is huge compared with the increase in program size. As the number of data points increases, the increase in speed is much lower than the increase in program size.

In a situation where execution speed is at a premium, it might be argued that even though the memory-speed exchange is nonlinear, it is still worthwhile, especially if large amounts of memory are available. One must be cautious, however, for program size and execution speed are not necessarily independent of each other (see Chapter 5), and if program size increases beyond a certain point, execution speed may actually go down on many machines. For these cases the heavy demands that the inline autogen method places on memory require-ments may prove prohibitive. A variation of the inline method attempts to alle-viate this problem and is described next.

6.2   INLINE SUBROUTINE CALLS

Observe that two kinds of computations are done in the Pfeifer-Blankinship algorithm. The first has the form $r = r + a(b+c)$; the second has the form $r = ab$, where a, b, c are points of the input data sequence. Morris calls these different operations *computational kernels*, or *ck*'s for short. It is a characteristic of many signal-processing algorithms that they consist of a few *ck*'s that are repeatedly executed. In the case of the Pfeifer-Blankinship algorithm, the two *ck*'s are rather simple.

Instead of creating a complete inline program, one can code each *ck* into a subroutine and create a program that calls the *ck*'s as needed. Next is such a program. The subroutines CORR1 and CORR2 are the two *ck*'s.

```
REAL      X(8)                    SUBROUTINE CORR1(I,J,K)
COMMON    X,R                     REAL      X(8)
CALL GET(X)                       COMMON    X,R
                                  R = R + (X(I)+X(J))*X(K)
R= 0.0                            RETURN
CALL CORR1(1,3,2)                 END
CALL CORR1(3,5,4)
CALL CORR1(5,7,6)                 SUBROUTINE CORR2(I,J)
CALL CORR2(7,8)                   REAL      X(8)
                                  COMMON    X,R
WRITE(*,*)'R(1) = ',R             R = R + X(I)*X(J)
RETURN                            RETURN
END                               END
```

This program does not contains loops or branches other than subroutine calls, so it can still be considered a sort of inline code program. In this particular example inline subroutine calls did not gain anything, for the program is longer and, because of the overhead of subroutine calls, slower. This is because the *ck*'s are simple single-line program statements. Typically the *ck*'s are multiline statements, and an inline subroutine program would be much shorter than an inline program.

6.3 THREADED CODE

While inline subroutine calls do result in shorter programs, they contain a large number of subroutine calls, and because of the overhead associated with this, it is not the most efficient approach. Threaded code and knotted code (discussed in the next section) are ingenious methods that eliminate the need for subroutine calls, but still retain much of the speed of inline code. It has its greatest value in applications where

- A program consists of a number of different computational kernels,
- Selection of the computational kernels is data-independent, and
- The program is executed repeatedly.

In a threaded code program an integer array, called a "thread," contains the order in which the ck's must be computed, as well as the data that the ck must operate on.

Refer back to the inline subroutine program of the previous section. The algorithm calls the first ck (CORR1) three times, and then calls the second ck (CORR2) once. On the first call to subroutine CORR1, it operates on elements number 1, 3, and 2 of the array X; on the second call on 3, 5, and 4; and on the third call on elements 5, 7, and 6 of X. Next subroutine CORR2 operates on elements 7 and 8 of X, and then the program terminates. The table below summarizes the information.

ck called	Element of X operated on.
1	1, 3, and 2
1	3, 5, and 4
1	5, 7, and 6
2	7,8
3 (exit)	-

An extra ck, number 3, was added, which is not really a ck but rather the exit point of the program. This table lies at the hart of a threaded code implementation, and the information contained in it stored in the thread array, called L in the following program. A COMPUTED GOTO statement is then used to access the array and, based on the contents of the thread, a particular ck is performed. No subroutine calls are made in this program, being replaced by precomputed jumps that are stored in the thread L. Next is the threaded code version of the autocorrelation computation:

```
REAL       X(8)      ┌─┬─┐──────── Elements of X that
INTEGER    L(16)     v v v         ck's must operate upon
DATA       L  / 1,1,3,2,
+                1,3,5,4,
+                1,5,7,6,
+                2,7,8,
+                3/
                     └──────────── This column is contains
CALL GET(X)                        the ck's that are to be
                                   executed
R = 0
I = 2
GOTO (1,2,3),L(I-1)

1    R = R + (X(L(I)) + X (L(I+1))) * X(L(I+2))  <──────── First ck
     I = I + 4
     GOTO (1,2,3),L(I-1)

2    R = R + X(L(I)) * X(L(I+1))     <──────── Second ck
     I = I + 3
     GOTO (1,2,3),L(I-1)

3    CONTINUE                    <──────── Third ck (exit)
     WRITE(*,*)'R(1) = ',R
     STOP
     END
```

This program computes only $r(1)$ of the autocorrelation sequence, but a program to compute the whole sequence would essentially be the same. The only difference would be that a larger thread L would be needed. Threaded code can substantially reduce the size of a program, but in some instances the thread array can still be too large. This leads to another hybrid program generation technique, discussed next.

6.4 KNOTTED CODE

Knotted code is based on the observation that a particular ck is often executed a number of times before the execution is transferred to another ck. In the present example, for instance, CORR1 is executed three times, then CORR2 is executed once, and then the program terminates. This is called a "knot" in the thread, and leads to a different approach to threaded code. Knots in the thread are nothing but the loops in the original algorithm. Because of the loops, the thread contains redundant information.

```
                           ┌─────────── This column contains the ck's
INTEGER    L(16) v                      that are to be executed
DATA       L  / 1,1,3,2,
+                1,3,5,4,
+                1,5,7,6,
+                2,7,8,
+                3/
```

To remove the redundant information, the thread is constructed to contain the *ck* to execute, followed by pointers (array indices) to the data to operate on. A sentinel is also placed in the thread array. After each invocation of the *ck*, a check is made to see if the sentinel has been reached. If not, the *ck* is executed again; or else execution moves on to the next *ck*. A good choice for the sentinel element is 0, for branch-on-zero instructions are quite efficient on most CPUs. Below is a knotted code version of the previous programs:

```
      REAL       X(8)            ┌────┬───── Sentinels
      INTEGER    L(8)            v    v
      DATA       L  /1,2,4,6,0,2,7,0/
                                 └────────── ck's to execute
      CALL GET(X)
C
      R = 0
      I = 2
1     R = R + X(L(I))*(X(L(I)+1) + X(L(I)-1))
      I = I + 1
      IF (L(I) .NE. 0) GOTO 1  <──────── Check for sentinel
C
      I = I + 2
2     R = R + X(L(I))*X(L(I)+1)
      I = I + 1
      IF (L(I) .NE. 0) GOTO 2  <──────── Check for sentinel

      WRITE(*,*)'R(1) =',R

      RETURN
      END
```

Note that the thread needed is much shorter than that of the threaded code program of the previous section.

6.5 INLINE CODE EXAMPLE

Nothing has yet been said on *how* to create the different types of programs discussed in this chapter. This section will show how to generate inline code. An existing program can be altered to function as an inline program generator by replacing each statement that operates on the input data with an appropriate WRITE statement. This altered program is then compiled and executed. Each statement that would usually operate on the data now writes to an output file, thus generating a new program. This may sound complicated, but is in fact quite simple. Shown below is an autogen program derived from the subroutine FFTA of Section 2.2. It is given here as a program and not as a subroutine, but it has basically the same structure as FFTA.

```
      WRITE(*,*)'PLEASE INPUT M'
      READ(*,*)M
      N = 2**M
      CALL GENFFT(N,M)
      STOP
      END
```

```
      SUBROUTINE GENFFT (N,M)
      COMPLEX    U,W
      WRITE(*,8)'SUBROUTINE FFTB(X)'
      WRITE(*,8)'COMPLEX X(',N,'),T'
      PI = 3.141592653589

C Bit Reversal.
      NV2 = N/2
      NM1 = N-1
      J  = 1
      DO 7 I = 1,NM1
         IF (I.GE.J) GOTO 5
             WRITE(*,8)'T      = X(',J,')'
             WRITE(*,8)'X(',J,') = X(',I,')'
             WRITE(*,8)'X(',I,') = T'
5            K = NV2
6     IF (K.GE.J) GOTO 7
             J = J-K
             K = K/2
         GOTO 6
7     J = J+K
8     FORMAT(7X,A,I3,A,I3,A)
9     FORMAT(7X,A,I3,A,F11.8,A,F11.8,A)

C Main part of FFT.
      DO 20 L= 1,M
         LE  = 2**L
         LE1 = LE/2
         U   = (1.0,0.)
         W   = CMPLX(COS(PI/LE1),SIN(PI/LE1))
         DO 20 J=1,LE1
            DO 10 I = J,N,LE
               IP   = I+LE1
               WRITE(*,9)'T=X(',IP,')*(',REAL(U),',',AIMAG(U),')'
               WRITE(*,8)'X(',IP,') = X(',I,') - T'
10             WRITE(*,8)'X(',I,') = X(',I,') + T'
20    U = U*W
      WRITE(*,8)'RETURN'
      WRITE(*,8)'END'
      RETURN
      END
```

The program was compiled and executed with $N = 8$ producing the next program. This program has no DO loops, IF statements, and each executable statement operates only on the data.

```
      SUBROUTINE FFTB(X)
      COMPLEX X( 8),T
      T     = X( 5)
      X( 5) = X( 2)
              :
      T = X( 2)*( 1.00000000, 0.00000000)
      X( 2) = X( 1) - T
              :
      T = X( 8)*(-0.70710670, 0.70710670)
      X( 8) = X( 4) - T
      X( 4) = X( 4) + T
      RETURN
      END
```

The following table shows the relative execution time and program (object) size for the two FFT subroutines on the IBM PS/2 model 30, running Microsoft FORTRAN.

N	t_{inline}/t_{normal} (coprocessor)	t_{inline}/t_{normal} (no coprocessor)	$Size_{inline}/Size_{normal}$
8	0.38	0.44	1.1
16	0.44	0.58	2.6
32	0.53	0.68	6.1
64	0.58	0.75	14.5
128	0.64	0.81	34.4

From the table it is clear that substantial savings in execution time can be accomplished for small N. Consider the case where a mathematical coprocessor is present. For N = 16 a $1/0.44 = 2.3$ times faster program comes at the expense of a 2.6 times larger program, which seems not too bad. It was mentioned previously that the memory-speed trade-off for inline code programs is usually nonlinear. This is borne out by the table. At N = 128 the size of the inline autogenerated program is about 34 times that of the regular program, and the speed is increased by a factor of only $1/0.64 = 1.6$. This is not unexpected, since the loop overhead becomes a smaller fraction of the total computation time as N increases.

With no coprocessor present, inline code again leads to a faster program, but with a somewhat smaller reduction in the execution speed. This is also expected, for mathematical operations are much more costly than loop overheads and control statements in the absence of a coprocessor, and inline code eliminates primarily the latter operations. It would seem possible to increase the efficiency of the autogenerated inline program further by including special WRITE statements for the cases where there are trivial multiplications. The statement

```
T = A(  2)
```

will then replace

```
T = A(  2)*( 1.00000000, 0.00000000).
```

However, most compilers will probably recognize the redundant multiplication and do the elimination anyway, so the program is best left as is.

The next table summarizes the measurements for the inline program on the Apollo DN4000 workstation, and the results are very different. The size of the inline code program is still much larger than FFTA, but for more than 16 data points inline code actually executes *slower* that FFTA. Even at N = 16 the improvement in execution speed is marginal and, with a 3.7 times larger program, certainly not worthwhile.

N	t_{inline}/t_{normal}	$Size_{inline}/Size_{normal}$
8	0.77	1.6
16	0.96	3.7
32	1.01	8.5
64	1.04	19.9
128	1.1	45.7

6.6 THREADED CODE EXAMPLE

In this section it is shown how to transform an existing program into a threaded code subroutine. Next is an implementation of a *prime factor algorithm* (PFA) FFT. It was derived from a subroutine by Burrus [34], and the reader is referred to that reference for the theory behind the algorithm. Note that the program is not complete, since the subroutines WFTA4 and WFTA5 are not listed.

```
        SUBROUTINE PFA(X,Y,N,M,NI)
        INTEGER    NI(4),I(16),
        INTEGER    IP(16),LP(16)
        REAL       X(*),Y(*)
C
        DO 40 K = 1,M
          N1 = NI(K)
          N2 = N/N1
          L  = 1
          N3 = N2-N1*(N2/N1)
          DO 10 J = 2,N1
            L = L+N3
            IF (L.GT.N1) L=L-N1
            LP(J) = L
10        CONTINUE
          DO 30 J = 1,N,N1
            IT  = J
            I(1) = J
            IP(1) = J
            DO 20 L=2, N1
              IT = IT+N2
              IF (IT.GT.N) IT=IT-N
              I(L)      = IT
              IP(LP(L)) = IT
20          CONTINUE
            GOTO(30,22,23,24,25),N1
22          CALL WFTA2(X,Y,I,IP)
            GOTO 30
23          CALL WFTA3(X,Y,I,IP)
            GOTO 30
24          CALL WFTA4(X,Y,I,IP)
            GOTO 30
25          CALL WFTA5(X,Y,I,IP)
30        CONTINUE
40      CONTINUE
        RETURN
        END
                (a)
```

```
        SUBROUTINE WFTA2(X,Y,I,IP)
        INTEGER    I(*),IP(*),
        REAL       X(*),Y(*)
C
        R1       = X(I(1))
        X(I(1))  = R1 + X(I(2))
        X(I(2))  = R1 - X(I(2))
        R1       = Y(I(1))
        Y(IP(1)) = R1 + Y(I(2))
        Y(IP(2)) = R1 - Y(I(2))
        RETURN
        END
                (b)

        SUBROUTINE WFTA3(X,Y,I,IP)
        INTEGER    I(*),IP(*)
        REAL       X(*),Y(*)
        PARAMETER  (C31=-0.86602540,
       +            C32=-1.5)
C
        R2       =(X(I(2))-X(I(3)))*C31
        R1       = X(I(2))+X(I(3))
        X(I(1))  = X(I(1))+R1
        R1       = X(I(1))+R1*C32
        S2       =(Y(I(2))-Y(I(3)))*C31
        S1       = Y(I(2))+Y(I(3))
        Y(I(1))  = Y(I(1))+S1
        S1       = Y(I(1))+S1*C32
        X(IP(2))= R1-S2
        X(IP(3))= R1+S2
        Y(IP(2))= S1+R2
        Y(IP(3))= S1-R2
        RETURN
        END
                (c)
                 :
                 :
```

The subroutine PFA accepts two arrays X and Y that hold the real and imaginary parts of data that must be transformed. The varaible N is the number of data points held in X and Y. The PFA is very efficient, but it has limitations on the length of the input data sequences. It is required (for this subroutine) that N be composed of mutually prime factors from the set of integers 2, 3, 4, 5. Thus, $N = 2 \times 5 = 10$ and $N = 3 \times 5 = 15$ are permissible, but $N = 2 \times 4 = 8$ is not, for 2 and 4 are not mutually prime. This particular implemcntation of the prime factor algorithm requires that along with N, the number of factors that make up N must be passed as M, and the individual factors must be stored in NI. For example, to transform a 10-point sequence, one would use:

```
NI(1) = 2
NI(2) = 5
M     = 2
CALL PFA(X,Y,N,M,NI)
```

Without getting into the theory of the PFA, one can see from the program listing that the PFA implementation centers around a few essential parts:

- Called subroutines WFTA2, WFTA3, WFTA4, WFTA5
- Computation of N1 used to branch with a COMPUTED GOTO, and
- Computation of arrays I and IP that are passed to the subroutines

The subroutines WFTA2, WFTA3, ... are clearly the computational kernels that are repeatedly executed, the variable N1 determines the sequence in which they are called, and the arrays I and IP determine on which data a called computational kernel will operate. Note that the calculation of N1, I, and IP is independent of the data arrays X and Y. Say one calculates the computational kernel calling sequence, as well as the data point sequence on an initialization run, and this information is stored in an array THREAD. Then one could rewrite the subroutine PFA in (a) above as PFASP:

```
        SUBROUTINE PFASP(X,Y)
        INTEGER    I(6,10)
        INTEGER    IP(6,10)
        INTEGER    THREAD(20)

        REAL       X(*),Y(*)
        COMMON     /MAPDAT/  I,IP,THREAD
        IMAP = 1
20      GOTO(30,22,23,24,25), THREAD(IMAP)
22          CALL WFTA2(X,Y,I(1,IMAP),IP(1,IMAP))
            GOTO 30
23          CALL WFTA3(X,Y,I(1,IMAP),IP(1,IMAP))
            GOTO 30
24          CALL WFTA4(X,Y,I(1,IMAP),IP(1,IMAP))
            GOTO 30
25          CALL WFTA5(X,Y,I(1,IMAP),IP(1,IMAP))
30          IMAP = IMAP + 1
        IF (THREAD(IMAP).GT.0) GOTO 20
        RETURN
        END
```

This is an abbreviated version of the original subroutine (in essence the last part). Note that IP and I have been changed from single to multidimensional arrays, and each subarray holds a set of integers. The subroutine PFASP above will produce the same results as PFA *if* the array THREAD holds the same sequence of integers as the N1's computed in the original subroutine, and the subarrays I(1,IMAP) and IP(1,IMAP) hold the same set of integers as I and IP held on each call in PFA.

This subroutine has none of the complex looping and branch calculations that PFA had, and should execute faster. The following subroutine INIT will initialize THREAD, I, and IP to their proper values:

```
      SUBROUTINE INIT(N,M,NI)
      INTEGER    NI(4),I(6,10),IP(6,10),LP(16)
      INTEGER    THREAD(20)
      COMMON     /MAPDAT/  I,IP,THREAD

      DO 5 K = 1,20
         THREAD(K) = 0
5     CONTINUE

      IMAP = 1
      DO 40 K = 1,M
         N1 = NI(K)
         N2 = N/N1
         L  = 1
         N3 = N2  - N1*(N2/N1)
         DO 10 J = 2, N1
            L = L + N3
            IF (L. GT. N1) L = L - N1
            LP(J) = L
10       CONTINUE
         DO 30 J = 1,N,N1
            IT    = J
            I(1,IMAP)  = J
            IP(1,IMAP) = J
            DO 20 L = 2, N1
               IT = IT + N2
               IF (IT.GT.N) IT = IT - N
               I(L,IMAP)       = IT
               IP(LP(L),IMAP) = IT
20          CONTINUE
            THREAD(IMAP) = N1
            IMAP  = IMAP + 1
30       CONTINUE
40    CONTINUE
      RETURN
      END
```

The subroutine is essentially the first part of the original subroutine, but instead of using computed values immediately, they are stored in arrays THREAD, I, and IP, which are held in a COMMON block MAPDAT. To use the new program, one must call INIT once with N, M, and NI set to the desired values, and then PFASP can be called repeatedly to transform data. If the number of data points N changes, INIT must be called again to set up the arrays THREAD, I, and IP properly. A typical program fragment might look like this:

```
              .
              :
      N = 30
      M = 3
      NI(1) = 3
      NI(2) = 2
      NI(3) = 5
      CALL INIT(N,M,NI)  <――――― Initialize thread
      DO 10 J=1, 50
          CALL GET(X,Y)  <――――― Get data
          CALL PFASP(X,Y) <――――― Transform
          .
          :
  10  CONTINUE           <――――― Get another set of data
          .
          :
```

Now for the big question. How much is gained by the conversion from the normal subroutine PFA to the special subroutine PFASP? Here are the results for a PC running Microsoft FORTRAN:

N	t_{thread}/t_{normal}	$Size_{thread}/Size_{normal}$
20	0.95	1.1
30	0.66	1.3
60	0.71	5.5

For $N = 20$ data points the 5% improvement in performance is marginal, but for $N = 30$ the threaded version of the PFA algorithm is $1/0.66 = 1.5$ times faster, albeit at the expense of a 30% larger executable program. Even at $N = 60$, the improvement is a substantial 30%, but the cost is a 5.5 times increase in program size. Many of the examples in this book show that array indexing on the Microsoft compiler is quite efficient compared to addition and multiplication, and this is once again underscored here. Because threaded code replaces program branches that are calculated at run-time with table look-up jumps and branches, the latter is more efficient.

On the Apollo, indexing is not as efficient, and one would not expect the threaded code version of the PFA to give major improvements in performance. This is indeed the case, as the next table for the Apollo shows:

N	t_{thread}/t_{normal}
20	0.94
30	0.98
60	1.04

Note that for $N = 20$ and $N = 30$ the improvement is marginal on the Apollo, and for $N = 60$ there is actually a decrease in performance. The results are even worse on the VAX and are summarized in the following table:

N	t_{thread}/t_{normal}
20	0.91
30	1.63
60	1.58

The reader may have noticed that the threaded code subroutine PFA differs from the threaded code discussed earlier, in that the ck calling sequence, and the data that a ck must operate on, are stored in different arrays. In the previous version of threaded code both were kept in the same array. This is not a major difference and is a natural result of the structure of the original algorithm. Another difference is that subroutine calls were used in the present example. This was done mainly to facilitate easy reading of the program listing.

The widely different results for the same programming technique again underscore the point that no one method for improving execution speed is guaranteed to work on all computers.

6.7 DISCUSSION

Of the different methods discussed in this chapter, the inline method is the simplest to implement, but in a sense also the most radical. Optimization is taken to the extreme. All loops are unwound, i.e., fully linearized; all program jumps and branches are coded into the generated subroutine; and all constants are precalculated. If memory allows, and if performance is not degraded because of caching and page faults, inline code is also the fastest method.

Between the inline method and the normal implementation of an algorithm lie different methods, each of which attempt to achieve the execution speed of inline code, but with the compactness of the normal implementation. The inline subroutine method is often a good compromise, for it is fairly fast and reasonably compact. Threaded code eliminates the subroutine call overhead, but is not so easy as inline and inline subroutine code to generate. It usually results in doubly indexed code, i.e., statements such as

```
R = R + X(L(I)) * X(L(I+1))
```

which may execute rather inefficiently on some computers. In some instances the thread size may be a problem, and knotted code should then be used. Knotted code may be the most complex of the methods but is also the closest to the original algorithm, for loops are allowed.

It is worth noting that one needs to know surprisingly little about the algorithm to be able to transform a program into a program generator. The examples in this chapter clearly illustrate this point. So while program generation may seem intimidating at first, it should not be. In many cases a programmer can start with a working, correct program and transform it systematically into a generator program, without detailed knowledge of the algorithm. Of course, familiarity with the algorithm will expedite the process.

7

INPUT/OUTPUT

Many programs are said to be input/output (I/O) bound, i.e., more time is spend on transferring data between the program and external files than on processing the data. This is because even a moderate amount of data transfer take a lot of time, and improving (I/O) efficiency will often solve the problem of a program that is too slow. Before discussing I/O efficiency any further, it is worth noting that I/O is a major source of portability problems among compilers, and this is especially true in the case of FORTRAN. The reasons for this are three-fold.

The first is that the FORTRAN 77 standard does not always completely specify all aspects of a particular I/O operation, and implementation is therefore left to the compiler writer. Second, the standard is sometimes confusing to users, and to compiler writers as well. Thus even "standard" elements of FORTRAN I/O often vary from system to system. Because of this, file I/O in FORTRAN is often a source of problems, even for seasoned programmers. For good review of the subject, the reader is referred to Jerrold Wagener's book [35]. The third reason is that I/O language extensions provided with FORTRAN compilers are usually very system-dependent, more so than, for instance, extensions to intrinsic functions, the latter often being quite portable. Consequently, techniques to improve I/O efficiency are also system-dependent, and earlier comments regarding the value of consulting one's compiler manual are particularly pertinent to I/O operations. Despite these problems, some general (and often very effective) methods apply to all systems, and are the topic of this chapter.

7.1   AN OVERVIEW OF FILE I/O

External files are either magnetic disks or tapes and, in some cases, optical media on which information is stored. To see how I/O operations influence efficiency, it is helpful to break down the process into steps:

- Position read/write head at the proper location,
- Write or read data, usually to or from an internal I/O buffer, and
- Perform possible format conversion of data during I/O

By reducing the time needed for each of these operations, one can speed up a program. The first step, positioning of the read/write head, is a relatively slow mechanical process. There are two possibilities. The first is finding a random record or block of data in a file, (this time is called the *average access time*). Typical values for hard disks vary from 150 msec down to 10 msec. The other possibility is a move to the next record, and since this is an incremental operation, it is much faster. Thus to improve I/O performance, transfer data as sequentially as possible.

Once the head is in the proper position, data is transferred to the I/O (read/write) buffer. The data transfer rate lies in the range of 1 - 1.5MB per second for current hard-disk technology. Data is usually transferred to the internal buffer not in single bytes, but in blocks the size of the buffer. This is because it is more efficient to read or write a block of bytes than to continually start and stop the read/write head. The size of the read/write buffer has an important influence on the efficiency of I/O; this will be dealt with in greater detail later. Once the buffer is full, subsequent I/O operations may or may not involve physical disk access, depending on whether the data referenced is already in the buffer, or still on disk or tape. Thus the program fragment:

```
CHARACTER*1   CH
    :
    :
READ(1,'(A)')CH
```

will read one byte from the buffer into the variable CH, or if the buffer is empty or all its elements already read, get a buffer of data from disk, and then assign CH to its proper value. The same argument holds for the FORTRAN BACKSPACE statement — it may or may not involve a physical disk head backspace. Note, however, that according to the VAX user's guide [36]:

> The backspace operation is not directly supported on most VAX I/O devices, including magnetic tape drives, and therefore must be simulated by rereading the input file from the beginning.

The user's guide then goes on to say that a buffering method to improve efficiency is used on the VAX, but that the operation is intrinsically inefficient and should be avoided.

7.2   FORMATTED VS UNFORMATTED I/O

The last stage during I/O is format conversion in the case of formatted files. This can be very time consuming, since for each element transferred, a conversion must be made from the machine's internal representation to the format specified by the program. This conversion is much more involved than one might realize at first, and the routines that perform this task are comparitively large and complex. Consequently, formatted I/O introduces a susbstantial overhead into a program in terms of size, as well as execution time.

Sometimes a programmer has no control over the format of the data, or the data must for some reason be stored formatted. For example, many image digitizers store the digitized images as a file of formatted integers. This makes it easy to read the images with any of a number of compilers. In these cases, formatted data transfer must be used. It is often worthwhile to preprocess the data by reading the formatted data file once, and then create an unformatted data file for future use. The formatted data file can then be compressed to save storage, and archived.

Generally speaking, then, formatted input and output are much slower than unformatted input and output. Thus, when the format is under the control of the programmer, unformatted I/O should be the first choice. Like most rules, however, this one also has exceptions, and in some instances *formatted*, not unformatted, data transfer is the most efficient. This will be discussed later in this section.

Often a whole array must be read from a file. This can be done with a DO loop or implied-DO loop, as in (a) below, where an unformatted read operation is performed:

```
REAL   Y(16000)                REAL   Y(16000)
   .                              .
   :                              :
READ(1)(Y(I),I=1,16000)        READ(1)Y

     (a)                            (b)
```

The READ statement and the implied-DO loop in (a) above actually constitute 16,000 different READ statements, each reading one value and then assigning it to the element of an array. One can also use array operands in READ and WRITE statements, as in (b). Now a single READ statement is executed, which is much faster.

Below are simple program fragments that write $4 \times 16,000 = 48,000$ bytes to an external file, first unformatted with an array operand, then unformatted with implied-DO looping, and finally formatted.

```
INTEGER  IDTA(16 000)
OPEN(1,FILE='TEST',FORM='UNFORMATTED')
WRITE(1)IDTA
CLOSE(1)
```
                                      (a)


```
INTEGER  IDTA(16 000)
OPEN(1,FILE='TEST',FORM='UNFORMATTED')
WRITE(1)(IDTA(I),I=1,16 000)
CLOSE(1)
```
                                      (b)


```
INTEGER  IDTA(16 000)
OPEN(1,FILE='TEST',FORM='FORMATTED')
WRITE(1,'(16 000I5)')(IDTA(I),I=1,16 000)
CLOSE(1)
```
                                      (c)

The next table shows $t_{(array)}/t_{form(I5)}$ and $t_{(DO\ loop)}/t_{form(I5)}$ for different compilers. In the table $t_{(array)}$ is the time to write 48,000 bytes with the unformatted array method as in (a) above, and $t_{(DO\ loop)}$ is the time to write 48,000 bytes unformatted with an implied-DO loop as in (b) above. Also, $t_{form(I5)}$ is the time to write 16,000 elements (4 bytes each) formatted with field width I5, as in (c) above.

Compiler	$t_{(array)}/t_{form(I5)}$	$t_{(DO\ loop)}/t_{form(I5)}$
Apollo	0.13	~1.1 *
Microsoft	0.15	0.15
Lahey	0.28	0.35
VAX	~0.01	~0.01

Except for the entry marked with the asterisk, the formatted output took substantially longer to complete than the unformatted write. (The asterisk entry is discussed in more detail in Section 7.3). This is a relatively small data file, and the few additional moments that it takes may not really matter. If a digitized picture of 1024 x 1024 were being input, an order of magnitude would certainly matter, and the unformatted method would most certainly be appreciated.

As another example, consider formatted vs unformatted read operations. Output files from image digitizers are often formatted files, for this makes transfer among different computer peripherals easier. For repeated processing of an image file, it is best to convert it to an unformatted file. That is the purpose of the next program, CONVERT. It reads the formatted file GIRLS.FMT, opens an unformatted file GIRLS.BIN, and then writes the contents of the formatted file to the unformatted file. Next it reopens and reads the file GIRLS.BIN, finally printing a few values as a quick check. Each read operation is also timed.

```
      PROGRAM   CONVERT
      INTEGER   PIC(128,128),NEWPIC(128,128)
      DOUBLE PRECISION T1,T2

C Read formatted file into array "PIC".
      CALL TIMER(T1)
      CALL TIMER(T1)
          OPEN(1,FILE='GIRLS.FMT',FORM='FORMATTED')
          DO 10 J = 1,128
             READ(1,'(128I4)')(PIC(I,J),I=1,128)
 10       CONTINUE
          CLOSE(1)
      CALL TIMER(T2)
      WRITE(*,*)'Formatted read time = ',T2-T1

C Write array: PIC unformatted to file "DTA".
      NBYTES=(4*128)*(4*128)
      OPEN(1,FILE='GIRLS.BIN',FORM='UNFORMATTED',RECL=NBYTES)
      WRITE(1)PIC
      CLOSE(1)

C Read unformatted file into array "NEWPIC"
      CALL TIMER(T1)
          NBYTES=(4*128)*(4*128)
          OPEN(4,FILE='GIRLS.BIN',FORM='UNFORMATTED',RECL=NBYTES)
          READ(4)NEWPIC
          CLOSE(4)
      CALL TIMER(T2)
      WRITE(*,*)'Unformatted read time = ',T2-T1

C Print a few values to check.
      DO 20 I = 1,5
         WRITE(*,*)NEWPIC(I,I)
 20   CONTINUE

      STOP
      END
```

The program was written to run on the Apollo DN4000 and calls the subroutine TIMER discussed in Section 3.2. For the Apollo compiler the RECL argument to the OPEN statement must be set for unformatted I/O. If the number of bytes transferred exceeds a certain limit (256 bytes), one should set RECL to the number of bytes. Next is the output from the program.

```
cdu> convert
 Formatted read time =  1.223399996757507
 Unformatted read time =  8.1972002983093260E-02
 1
 70
 107
 110
 116
Fortran STOP
```

The results show that the difference between the two different read operations is dramatic, and the unformatted method is about 15 times faster than the formatted method. So both read and write operations are much more efficient if performed unformatted.

Unformatted input and output have two other benefits. First, because no format conversions are made during I/O, the internal precision of the machine is preserved during data transfer. This is important for real variables. The second is that the files created with unformatted I/O are often smaller than the formatted files. For example, the size of file TEST with the unformatted write should be about 16,000 x 4 = 64,000 bytes, for each array element is 4 bytes. On the other hand, the formatted version of TEST's size, written with an I5 field width should be about 16,000 x 5 = 80,000 bytes. Of course, if the field width were I3, the size would be smaller, about 48,000 bytes. In practice, file sizes differ slightly from these values, for some additional housekeeping information is written to the files.

It was mentioned before that unformatted data transfer is often, but not always, faster. Consider a program running on a microcomputer that transfers data to and from a floppy disk, and that this makes the program input/output bound. One's first instinct is to use unformatted read and write operations to improve run-time. However, it is the physical read/write operations that make I/O for the floppy disk so slow, and not the format conversion. To improve data transfer it may be best to use formatted I/O, for this can reduce the total amount of data transferred.

Returning to the previous example, if the file TEST is on a floppy disk, one can safely neglect the effect of format conversion. The formatted write should take about 48,000/64,000 = 75% of the time it takes to perform the unformatted write, and actual measurements confirm this. If, on the other hand, the file is located on a fast hard disk, format conversion will be the bottleneck, and formatted I/O will be slower. Measurements again support this— on a 28 msec hard disk, the formatted transfer took almost three times as long to complete as the unformatted write operation.

7.3 IMPLIED-DO LOOP COLLAPSING

Refer back to the table of the previous section. It shows that for the Microsoft compiler, as well as the VAX, the two unformatted WRITE operations

```
WRITE(1)(DTA(I),I=1,16 000)
```

and

```
WRITE(1)DTA
```

took identical times to complete. One would expect that because the implied-DO loop consists of 16,000 different write operations, it should take longer. However, the 16,000 items written to the file are consecutive elements of an array. These two compilers recognized that the implied-DO loop WRITE performs the same task as the array method WRITE, and selected the faster of the two operations during compilation. This is called *implied-DO loop collaps-*

ing, and is often done as a matter of course for (unformatted) I/O of one-dimensional arrays. One cannot *assume* implied-DO loop collapsing, however. The table entry for the Apollo, marked with an asterisk, shows that the implied-DO loop unformatted write took about 10% *longer* than even the formatted write, which is somewhat surprising. The Lahey compiler also did not collapse the implied-DO loop.

Implied-DO loop collapsing is also possible in the case of multidimensional arrays, *if* array subscripts are referenced in the proper order:

```
REAL   Y(100,50)              REAL  Y(100,50)
  .                             .
  :                             :
N = 100                       N = 100
M = 50                        M = 50
READ(1)((Y(I,J),I=1,N),J=1,M) READ(1)((Y(I,J),J=1,M),I=1,N)

        (a)                           (b)
```

The code shown in (a) reads the array elements in the order that they are in memory (see Chapter 5), and an optimizing compiler should collapse at least the M inner loops. The code in (b) does not read the data in its natural order, and N x M = 5000 READs are performed, making it slower.

Input/output statements that contain mathematical expressions are often not collapsed, and this will reduce I/O efficiency. In (a) below, before an integer array IDATA is written unformatted to a file, a mathematical operation is performed on each element of the array. The code fragment in (b) performs the same task, but now the mathematical operations performed on the array and the WRITE are done in two steps.

```
      INTEGER     IDATA(16000)
      PARAMETER   (N = 16000)
        .
        :
C Perform mathematical operation on IDATA during WRITE.
      WRITE(1)((IDATA(I)*IDATA + 15*IDATA(I) + 1),I = 1,N)
        .
        :
                        (a)


      INTEGER     IDATA(16000)
      PARAMETER   (N = 16000)
        .
        :
C Perform mathematical operation on IDATA separately.
      DO 10 I = 1, N
          IDATA(I) = IDATA(I)*IDATA(I) + 15*IDATA(I) + 1
   10 CONTINUE
      WRITE(1)(IDATA(I),I = 1,N)
        .
        :
                        (b)
```

The next table summarizes the difference in execution speed of the code in (a) and the code in (b). Note the increase in efficiency, except in the case of the Lahey compiler, which does not perform implied-DO loop collapsing anyway. The Apollo compiler again produces a surprise; it too does not perform implied-DO loop collapsing, but efficiency is nonetheless increased by not combining the WRITE operation with the mathematical operation on the data.

Compiler	t_b/t_a
Apollo	0.91
Microsoft	0.30
Lahey	~1.0
VAX	0.33

The preceding discussion focused on transferring data to an external file, but a similar rule applies to READ operations, i.e., to improve efficiency, keep mathematical operations and data transfer from an external file separate if possible.

7.4 RUN-TIME FORMATTING

In some instances the format of a file is not known prior to program execution. For example, a graphics program that reads data from a file and then displays it might be expected to accept a variety of file formats. A method of treating a situation like this is to precede the data in a file with a *file header* that contains pertinent information about the file, including the format of the data. In FORTRAN, the format specifier used during I/O can take on a number of forms, including character expressions. One can use this to dynamically specify formats for read/write operations.

As an illustration, consider the program fragment below. It opens a file TT.DAT and then creates a format in the character variable FMT. Next, the file header, consisting of the number of data points NX and the format FMT, is written to the file. Finally, NX data points are written according to the format specified by FMT, and the file is closed.

```
INTEGER        DTA(500)
CHARACTER*10   FMT
      .
      :
NX = 20
OPEN(1,FILE='TT.DAT')
WRITE(FMT,'(A,I4,A)')'('(',NX,'I5)'   <——— Generate header
WRITE(1,'(I4,A)')NX,FMT               <——— Write file header
WRITE(1,FMT)(DTA(I),I=1,NX)           <——— Write data
CLOSE(1)
      .
      :
```

Here is how TT.DAT might look:

```
20(  2015)
   1    4    9   16   25   36   49   64   81  100  121  ...
```

The first line is the file header, and the second contains the 20 data points, each formatted as I5. To read the file, a program must open TT.DAT, then get the file header to obtain the number of data points as well as their format. The format specification is then used to read the data. Next is a program fragment that implements these ideas:

```
INTEGER          DTA(500)
CHARACTER*10     FMT,FNAME

WRITE(*,*)'File name?'
READ(*,*)FNAME
OPEN(1,FILE = FNAME)
READ(1,'(I4,A10)')NX,FMT     <——— Read file header to obtain format
READ(1,FMT)(DTA(I),I=1,NX)   <——— Read file
CLOSE(1)
   .
   :
```

This method works fine, but it has two limitations. First, for a program to perform run-time formatting, the compiler has to include calls to routines that scan and decode the character expressions. This increases the size of the generated programs, often substantially. Second, the format specification contained in the character variable FMT above must be decoded during execution, while the format specification in

```
READ(1,'(2015)')(DTA(I),I=1,NX)
```

can be decoded during compilation. One should therefore attempt to avoid run-time formatting if possible.

One possible method is to specify a number of different formats in the source file. These formats are then decoded by the compiler during compilation. During execution the program then chooses which format to use. While this may not be as flexible as the previous method, it is faster. If run-time formatting must be used, try to eliminate as many blanks as possible from the character expression that holds the format. For example, if FMT is a character variable, then

```
FMT = '    20 (    2015)  '
```

is less efficient than

```
FMT = '20(2015)'
```

This is because the blanks in the first statement must be removed during program execution.

7.5 DATA REORGANIZATION

Often only certain elements of an array must be transferred to external storage; the code fragment in (a) below writes every second element of the array DTA to an external file. Because no implied-DO loop collapsing (see Section 7.3) is possible, 5000 write operations are performed.

```
       INTEGER      DTA(10000)                    INTEGER    DTA(10000),ITEMP(5000)
         .                                          .
         :                                          :
       NX = 1000                                  J=1
       WRITE(1)(DTA(i),I=1,NX,2)                  DO 10 i = 1,NX,2
         .                                            ITEMP(j) = DTA(i)
         :                                            j=j+1
                                               10 CONTINUE
                                                  WRITE(1)ITEMP
                                                    .
                                                    :
              (a)                                      (b)
```

In (b) an auxiliary array ITEMP is defined, and every second element of DTA is copied to this array; then ITEMP is written to the external file with a single WRITE statement. The number of write operations are thus reduced by 4999, but at the expense of larger storage (the array ITEMP). The effect can be dramatic, as the next table shows.

Compiler	$t_{reorder}/t_{normal}$
Apollo	0.15
Microsoft	0.25
Lahey	0.92
VAX	~1.1

In some instances one might not even need auxiliary storage. If preservation of DTA is of no concern, a programmer can put the EQUIVALENCE statement to good use. The strategy is to define an auxiliary array, and EQUIVALENCE it with the first part of DTA. The program then copies every second element of DTA to this auxiliary array. Because of the EQUIVALENCE statement, however, the data is really copied to the first part of DTA itself, so the contents of DTA are not preserved. This is illustrated in (a):

```
       INTEGER       DTA(10000),  ITEMP(5000)
       EQUIVALENCE   (DTA,ITEMP)
         .
         :
       J=1
       DO 10 I = 1,NX,2
          ITEMP(J) = DTA(I)
          J=J+1
   10  CONTINUE
       WRITE(1)ITEMP

              (a)
```

In principle the EQUIVALENCE statement is not needed, and code fragment in (b) below performs the same function by copying the required data to the beginning of the array DTA, and then writing the data to the external file with an implied-DO loop. On compilers that perform implied-DO loop collapsing, (a) and (b) execute equally fast. On compilers that do not perform implied-DO loop collapsing, the code in (b) is slower than that in (a). The code in (a) is also somewhat more explicit in its purpose.

```
      INTEGER     DTA(10000)
         .
         .
      J=1
      DO 10 I = 1,NX,2
         DTA(J) = DTA(I)
         J=J+1
   10 CONTINUE
      WRITE(1)(DTA(I),I=1,5000)
         .
         .

                       (b)
```

7.6 DATA REDUCTION

The discussion thus far has centered on transferring data between a program and external storage. Programs must communicate with other peripherals as well, e.g., plotters and printers. In applications such as the plotting and printing of graphs, it is often possible to substantially reduce plotting time by reducing the amount of data transferred. An excellent example of this is described by Richard Fowell and David McNiel [37]. They argue among other things that

> Plots are only approximate. There is little point in trying to plot a curve to more accuracy than the resolution of the plot device.

This observation is analogous to the accuracy-speed trade-off discussed in Section 2.5, and is the rationale behind a *fan compression* algorithm that they describe in detail in their article. The algorithm greatly reduces the number of data points sent to a laser printer (or any other plotting device) and, according to the authors, tripled their department's laser print speed for plots with many points. The description of the fan compression algorithm is somewhat involved, and the original article contained a small publishing error [38], but the implementation of the algorithm consists of a mere 55 lines of straightforward FORTRAN, a worthwhile investment for tripling the effective print speed.

A surprising number of programming tasks involve text processing, and quite often processing of program files. One example is converting nonstandard FORTRAN constructs such as DO-WHILE and DO-ENDDO to standard FORTRAN to make programs portable. Another example is processing source files to achieve a consistent source code format, so-called pretty-printing. One can frequently reduce the size of text files by replacing repeated blanks with tab characters. This will, for example, typically result in reductions of 15-25% in file sizes for FORTRAN programs. Smaller files mean faster I/O from disk files, faster compilation, as well as faster printing. It is usually much more efficient for a printer to advance to the next tab stop than to print a number of spaces.

Below is a code fragment that "entabs" a character variable called LINE. The integer function LEN_TRIM is not shown, but it simply returns the non-blank length of its argument, i.e., LEN_TRIM(' 123 ') is equal to four. The code entabs all spaces, and must be altered to handle quoted strings in FORTRAN.

```
      CHARACTER        LINE*72,BLANKS*10
      PARAMETER        (ITAB = 9,NBLNK = 4)
         :
      BLANKS = ' '

      CALL GET(LINE)          <————— Get character line
      LL = LEN_TRIM(LINE)    <————— Get  nonblank length of LINE
      K = 1
      I = 1
10    IF (LINE(I:I+NBLNK-1) .EQ. BLANKS(1:NBLNK)) THEN
          LINE(K:K+1) = CHAR(ITAB) <————————— Replace blanks with tab
          I = I+NBLNK-1
      ELSE
          LINE(K:K) = LINE(I:I)
      ENDIF
      K = K + 1
      I = I + 1
      IF (.NOT. (I.GT.LL)) GOTO 10
C  At this point LINE(1:K-1) contains the entabbed line.
      WRITE(*,'(1X,A)')LINE(1:K-1)
         :
```

A companion program can be written to "detab" text files, in other words, replace tab characters with a fixed number of spaces.

7.7 I/O BUFFER SIZE

The I/O buffer size influences the efficiency of data transfer. For instance, if the buffer size is 256 bytes, then four read operations are needed to transfer 1024 bytes from an external file. With a buffer size equal to or larger than 1024, only one read operation is needed. Standard FORTRAN not does provide the capability to specify the size of the I/O buffer, but most compilers provide some control through language extensions. On the VAX and Microsoft compilers, buffer or block size is controlled with the OPEN statement. For example, the statement

```
      OPEN(1,FILE='TEST',STATUS='NEW',BLOCKSIZE=8192)
```

opens a new file TEST and sets the block size used for data transfer to 8192 bytes. This matches the size of the physical blocks on magnetic tape on the VAX. Even though a user may request a specific buffer or block size, compilers assign block sizes in system-dependent units. So if the basic unit on a system is 512 bytes, and a program requests a block size of 2000 bytes, the compiler sets the block size as the closest multiple of 512, namely, 2048.

To get an idea how the block size affects data transfer, refer to the next table. It shows the relative unformatted write time of 64,000 bytes of a program running Microsoft FORTRAN on a microcomputer. The average access time of the hard disk on the PC was 28 msec.

Block size (bytes)	t_{block}/t_{normal}
512	1
1024	0.52
2048	0.26
4096	0.20
8192	0.13

By doubling the buffer size from 512 to 1024 bytes, the data transfer rate was roughly doubled ($1/0.52 \sim 2$). Doubling the buffer size again also doubled the transfer rate. But increasing the buffer size from 2048 to 4096 bytes did not increase the data transfer rate correspondingly. This illustrates a general rule: increasing the buffer size will increase the transfer rate, but beyond some point the increase in transfer rate becomes less than the increase in buffer size.

While larger buffers improve I/O operations, they also require more memory at execution time. In many cases the buffers are allocated as the files are opened and then deallocated as the files are closed. So if large buffers create memory problems, try to limit the number of files that are open simultaneously.

On some compilers a programmer can request multiple I/O buffers. On the VAX, for instance, the statement

```
OPEN(UNIT=1,FILE='TEST',FORM='UNFORMATTED',BUFFERCOUNT=3)
```

opens a file TEST, and requests three read/write buffers. Multiple buffers allow a program to perform some I/O concurrently with other operations. Normally when a program writes to a buffer, and the buffer becomes full, the program halts while the buffer contents are transferred to an external storage device. With multiple buffers, the program simply uses the next buffer while writing the previous buffer to external storage. Total program efficiency can be increased, but more buffers need more memory. Increase in program efficiency is also highly dependent on the particular applications, so some experimentation is in order.

7.8 SYSTEM-DEPENDENT ROUTINES

Many compilers provide users with a complete set of I/O routines that are specifically tailored to the particular compiler and hardware. Fairly widespread is *asynchronous* I/O provided in various forms on many machines. This type of I/O provides the facility to perform some data transfer to and from the program's data buffers while the program is executing normally. This is somewhat analogous to multiple buffers, and because program execution and data transfer are performed in parallel, total program efficiency is increased. Depending on the particular application, asynchronous read/write operations can provide a marked improvement in program execution time.

While system-dependent routines provide optimum I/O control, they are obviously nonportable, but it was noted at the beginning of this chapter that FORTRAN I/O is often nonportable anyway. It is also often possible to keep all I/O operations localized to a small number of routines, so that a program may be ported with little code rewriting. So portability may not be an overriding concern when it comes to using system-dependent I/O routines.

7.9 SUMMARY

This chapter addressed some issues that bear on file input/output operations. It is important, because some programs spend a large amount of time on input/output operations. Just as the presence of a mathematical coprocessor influences programming strategy, so does the type of external storage determine which I/O operations will be most effective. If the files are located on fast external storage devices such as hard disks, format conversion takes up most of the time, and unformatted data transfer is preferable, even if it involves more data.

If the files are located on relatively slow external storage devices such as magnetic tape and floppy disks, format conversion may make up but a small part of the total transfer time. In such cases one should reduce the total amount of data transfer by compressing data, or even by performing formatted input/output. In all cases, perform data transfer in as large blocks, and as sequentially as possible, for this will ensure the most efficient use of the hardware.

Finally, maximal performance for a particular hardware configuration is often only obtained by using nonstandard FORTRAN extensions, or installation-dependent input/ouput routines, so a programmer has to choose between performance and portability.

8

GENERAL TECHNIQUES

This chapter is devoted to miscellaneous techniques for improving the execution speed of FORTRAN programs.

8.1 INTRINSIC AND STATEMENT FUNCTIONS

The use of intrinsic functions is highly recommended. They enhance readability of the code, minimize portability problems, and in many cases lead to faster, more compact code. The reason for this is that they are invariably implemented in the computer's machine language, and are in many cases even hardware-implemented. Some intrinsic functions are treated as macros by compilers in that every occurrence of the intrinsic function in the source file is substituted with inline machine language instructions. This process is referred to as *inline expansion* of the intrinsic function. The functions that are usually treated this way are:

```
INT,     REAL,    DBLE,
CMPLX,   AINT,    AIMAG,
CONJ,    SIGN,    ABS,
MOD,     MAX,     MIN
```

Many compilers allow some control through compiler switches over which of these and other functions are treated as true functions, and which functions are expanded as inline code. It is often worthwhile to do some experimentation. Because inline code does not have the overhead of a function call, it is faster, but usually results in larger executable files.

Next is a fragment of the routine ATOI2 from Section 2.1 The statement function ISDIGIT returns .TRUE. if its argument is a digit and .FALSE. otherwise. Most compilers treat statement functions as macros and generate inline code for each reference of the function. A programmer can therefore use them to good effect to increase modularity and readability of a program without sacrificing efficiency.

```
        INTEGER FUNCTION ATOI2 (STRING)
        CHARACTER*(*)    STRING,C*1

C Statement function: ISDIGT returns .TRUE. if argument is a digit.
        LOGICAL          ISDIGT
        ISDIGT(C) = (LGE(C,'0') .AND. LLE(C,'9'))
                  :
                  :
  20    IF (ISDIGT (STRING(I:I))) THEN
            ATOI2 = 10*ATOI2 + ICHAR(STRING(I:I)) - ICHAR ('0')
            I = I + 1
        GOTO 20
        ENDIF
        ATOI2 = S*ATOI2
        RETURN
        END
```

8.2 SUBROUTINE LIBRARIES

There are some excellent libraries available to the FORTRAN programmer, e.g., the IMSL libraries published by the Association for Computing Machinery (ACM). The ACM distribution service [39] is an invaluable source of FORTRAN source code, and these routines are very portable, for routines submitted must pass a portability test before being accepted for publication. The use of such libraries has several advantages. First, the routines contained in these libraries reflect current research on a particular problem. Second, they are often widely available on a large number of machines, ranging from large mainframes, to "best of" versions for microcomputers. A programmer therefore has access to a large number of prewritten routines, without losing too much program portability. Third, library routines can be very efficient, for a library found on a particular system has often been specifically adapted to the machine's architecture.

8.3 LANGUAGE EXTENTIONS

Most FORTRAN compilers implement several extensions to the FORTRAN language, and some of them were mentioned in this book. One should distinguish between two types of language extensions. The first type is mainly cosmetic. For example, modern control structures such as DO-WHILE, DO-ENDDO, and so on, are easily converted to standard FORTRAN. These cosmetic extensions therefore seldom present serious portability problems.

The second kind of extension includes recursion, data structures (such as records), pointer manipulation, and nonstandard intrinsic functions. Some of these extensions are so common among compilers that they are almost de facto FORTRAN 77, and a programmer can use them with little loss to portability. If used properly, they can improve performance of selected parts of a program substantially. An example is the so-called bit-manipulation functions, some of which are:

Description	Apollo	Microsoft	Lahey	VAX
Bitwise AND	AND	IAND	IAND	IAND
Bitwise OR	OR	IOR	IOR	IOR
Complement	-	NOT	NOT	NOT
Bit test	-	BTEST	-	BTEST
Bit set	-	IBSET	-	IBSET
Logical shift	-	ISHFT	-	ISHFT

To understand how to use bit-manipulation functions in a program, consider the binary representation of integers:

$$12_{10} = 01100_2$$
$$24_{10} = 11000_2$$
$$6_{10} = 00110_2$$

$$13_{10} = 01101_2$$
$$7_{10} = 00111_2$$
$$27_{10} = 11011_2$$

(a)

even integers

(b)

odd integers

Note that the bit pattern of 24 is identical to that of 12, except for a left shift by one position. The same holds for $26 = 2 \times 13$, and it is generally true that multiplication by 2 is identical to shifting the bit pattern left by 1. On most (probably all) CPUs the latter operation is much faster. Also, the bit pattern for $6 = 12/2$ is a right-shifted version of the bit pattern of 12, and division by 2 is in general identical to a single right shift. For the (odd) integer 13, a right shift resulted in 6, which is identical to FORTRAN integer division (division followed by truncation) 13/2.

Multiplication or division of integers by factors of 2 is therefore equivalent to left or right shifts of the bit patterns, and in some cases faster. Most FORTRAN compilers have the bit shift function (usually) called ISFHT(N,M), which returns the variable N's bit pattern shifted M times, so that

```
N = 14
WRITE(*,*)ISHFT(N, 1)
WRITE(*,*)ISHFT(N, 2)
WRITE(*,*)ISHFT(N, 3)
WRITE(*,*)ISFHT(N,-1)
WRITE(*,*)ISHFT(N,-2)
```

will print the numbers 28, 56, 112, 7, and 3.

The reason why bit shifting is not always faster is that the number of clock cycles for integer multiplication and division does not depend on the operands. For example, to multiply N with 6 takes just as long as to multiply N with 60. On the other hand, the number of clock cycles needed for shifting an integer do depend on the amount of shift. So it might be best to divide and multiply in some instances, and to perform shift operations in other instances. Where the cutoff point occurs is machine-dependent, and a programmer should not attempt to perform multiplications by using bit-shift functions in the source code. It is the task of the compiler to figure out when to replace operations with shifts.

A good application for bit-manipulation functions is testing for odd or even integers. First, consider how this is done in standard FORTRAN 77, which does not have the capability to test individual bits. Normal practice is to divide the integer by 2 and check the remainder. If the remainder is zero, the integer is even, otherwise the integer is odd. FORTRAN's MOD function can be used to accomplish the same, and to determine if an integer N is even, test if MOD(N,2) is equal to zero. Alternatively, if MOD(N,2) is not zero, N is odd. Here are two functions that use these ideas:

```
LOGICAL FUNCTION ISEVEN(N)          LOGICAL FUNCTION ISODD(N)
C                                    C
C Returns .TRUE. If N even.         C Returns .TRUE. If N odd.
C                                    C
  IF (MOD(N,2).EQ.0) THEN             IF (MOD(N,2).NE.0) THEN
     ISEVEN = .TRUE.                     ISODD = .TRUE.
  ELSE                                ELSE
     ISEVEN = .FALSE.                    ISODD = .FALSE.
  ENDIF                               ENDIF
  RETURN                              RETURN
  END                                 END

        (a)                                  (b)
```

To see how bit-manipulation functions are used, refer back to the bit patterns of integers. Note that the odd integers always have a 1 in the rightmost position, and the even integers always have a zero in that position. Therefore, to test for odd/even, one need only examine the rightmost bit of an integer. A nonstandard function found on many FORTRAN compilers is the IAND(N,M) function. This function returns the numeric value of the bitwise AND of its integer arguments N and M. For instance, if $N = 6_{10} = 110_2$ and $M = 3_2 = 011_2$, then IAND(N,M) = 2. To test the rightmost bit in N, one can use IAND($N,1$), and if IAND($N,1$) is zero, N is even, otherwise N is odd. Shown next are much faster implementations of the two functions above, where the nonstandard IAND function has been employed:

```
      LOGICAL FUNCTION ISEVEN(N)                    LOGICAL FUNCTION ISODD(N)
C                                             C
C Returns .TRUE. If N even.                   C Returns .TRUE. If N odd.
C                                             C
      IF (IAND(N,1).EQ.0) THEN                     IF (IAND(N,1).EQ.1) THEN
         ISEVEN = .TRUE.                              ISODD = .TRUE.
      ELSE                                         ELSE
         ISEVEN = .FALSE.                             ISODD = .FALSE.
      ENDIF                                        ENDIF
      RETURN                                       RETURN
      END                                          END
                  (a)                                         (b)
```

One will probably not use the functions above, but rather code them inline into a program. For an example, consider the determination of the greatest common divisor gcd(u,v) of two integers u and v. Knuth [40] details the following algorithm:

Step 1: Set gcd$=1$, and then repeatedly set gcd$=$gcd$*2$, $u=u/2$, and $v=v/2$, zero or more times until one of u and v is odd.

Step 2: If u is odd , set $t=-v$, and go to step 4, else set $t=u$.

Step 3: Set $t=t/2$.

Step 4: If t is even, go to step 3.

Step 5: If $t>0$, set $u=t$, else set $v=-t$.

Step 6: Set $t=u-v$. If t not zero go to step 3, else gcd$=u*$gcd, and the algorithm terminates.

This algorithm is called the *binary gcd algorithm*, for it is quite suited to binary arithmetic. Because of this, Knuth claims that if implemented in his MIX assembly language, this algorithm is about 20% faster than Euclid's algorithm, the standard way of calculating the gcd of two numbers. Next is a fairly direct implementation of the binary gcd algorithm in standard FORTRAN, and the statement labels correspond to the steps in the algorithm. Note, however, that one must use the MOD function to test for odd or even integers, for bit-manipulation functions are not part of standard FORTRAN.

```
      INTEGER FUNCTION GCDBIN(U,V)
      INTEGER U,V,T

      GCDBIN = 1
1     IF ((MOD(U,2).NE.0).OR.(MOD(V,2).NE.0)) GOTO 2
         U   = U/2
         V   = V/2
         GCDBIN=GCDBIN*2
```

```
        GOTO 1
2       IF (MOD(U,2).NE.0) THEN
            T = -V
        GOTO 4
        ELSE
            T = U
        ENDIF
3       T = T/2
4       IF (MOD(T,2).EQ.0) GOTO 3
5       IF (T.GT.0) THEN
            U = T
        ELSE
            V = -T
        ENDIF
6       T = U - V
        IF (T.NE.0) GOTO 3
        GCDBIN=U*GCDBIN
        RETURN
        END
```

With bit-manipulation functions available as extensions to FORTRAN 77, one can use IF(IAND(U,1).EQ.1) to test if the variable U is odd, and the implementation becomes:

```
        INTEGER FUNCTION GCDBIN(U,V)
        INTEGER U,V,T
C
        GCDBIN = 1
1       IF ((IAND(U,1).EQ.1).OR.(IAND(V,1).EQ.1)) GOTO 2
            U = U/2
            V = V/2
            GCDBIN = GCDBIN*2
        GOTO 1
2       IF (IAND(U,1).EQ.1) THEN
            T = -V
        GOTO 4
        ELSE
            T = U
        ENDIF
3       T = T/2
4       IF (IAND(T,1).EQ.0) GOTO 3
5       IF (T .GT. 0) THEN
            U = T
        ELSE
            V = -T
        ENDIF
6       T = U - V
        IF (T.NE.0) GOTO 3
        GCDBIN = U*GCDBIN
        RETURN
        END
```

Division by two was not replaced with bit-shift functions for the reasons outlined before, and the altered statements are the lines labeled 1, 2, and 4. The next table summarizes $t_{F77(ext)}/t_{F77}$, where the $t_{F77(ext)}$ is the time for computing gcd(40902,24140) with the FORTRAN plus extensions implementation, and t_{F77} is the execution time of the standard FORTRAN version. It clearly shows that an important increase in speed resulted from using nonstandard functions.

Compiler	$t_{F77(ext)}/t_{F77}$
Apollo	0.63
Microsoft	0.58
Lahey	0.63
VAX	0.43

It is instructive to compare the execution speed of the supposedly fast binary gcd algorithm with Euclid's algorithm for finding the gcd of two integers. Below is an implementation of the latter:

```
        INTEGER FUNCTION GCDEUC(U,V)
        INTEGER U,V,R
10      IF (V .NE. 0) THEN
            R = MOD(U,V)
            U = V
            V = R
        GOTO 10
        ENDIF
        GCDEUC=U
        RETURN
        END
```

The algorithm is very simple and should be fairly fast. This is indeed the case, as the next table (again for calculating cgd(40920,24140)) shows:

Compiler	$t_{F77(ext)}/t_{Euclid}$
Apollo	0.94
$MS_{(NO87)}$	1.93
$MS_{(87)}$	1.93
Lahey	2.60
VAX	1.26

In the table $t_{F77(ext)}$ is the execution time for the binary algorithm implemented with the FORTRAN language extensions, and t_{Euclid} is the execution time for GCDEUC shown above. The table shows that Euclid's algorithm is faster than the binary algorithm on the microcomputers, and the binary algorithm is only marginally faster on the Apollo workstation. So while the binary algorithm is more efficient in Knuth's MIX assembly language, it does not seem worthwhile in FORTRAN.

8.4 ASSEMBLY LANGUAGE

When really high speed is required, parts of a program can be programmed in the computer's machine language. It is rarely necessary, however, and not so easy to improve on a compiler. Says Jeff Dunteman, a well-known author and contributor to microcomputer magazines [41]:

Five years of crawling through native code HLL (high-level language) programs with a debugger have convinced me of this: Modern high-level languages write better assembly language that 99 percent of all the programmers who have ever lived or will ever live. Not only are your chances of writing faster code than the compiler not good, the chances are excellent that your own assembly language will be slower.

This sentiment applies not only to microcomputer compilers, but to other compilers as well. It is true that assembly language programs can be very efficient, but by using assembler one is making the program less portable. That is, the program using assembler routines cannot be used on a computer that uses another type of CPU. Also, writing any sizable assembly language program is very tedious business. Fortunately it is seldom required to code more than a few critical sections of a program in assembler.

When one has decided that portability is less important than speed it might be worthwhile to use language extensions (see previous section) instead. The reason is that it is much easier to use high-level language extensions than to use assembly language. Also, some language extensions are very similar from compiler to compiler, so that altering code to run on different computers may be relatively simple.

9

EXAMPLE: POLYGON FILLING

This is the first of two chapters in which larger examples are discussed. In this chapter the problem of filling the interior of a polygon efficiently is examined, and in the next chapter a subroutine that can be used to perform file compression is developed and then systematically optimized.

An important problem in computer graphics is that of filling the interior of polygons. A routine that will perform this task is typically called many times in a graphics program. It should therefore be as efficient as possible. Various filling techniques, exist, which include *flood filling*, as well as an important incremental method, called the scan line algorithm. Flood filling is discussed only briefly in this chapter, but an implementation of the *scan-line algorithm* is presented in some detail.

9.1 SOME DEFINITIONS

Before discussing some of the polygon fill algorithms, it is useful to define the concept of the convexity of a polygon. If the line that connects any two points that lie inside a polygon, is completely inside the polygon, the polygon is said to be *convex*. A special case of convexity is polygons that are *horizontally convex*. In this case it is required that if any two points inside the polygon have the same *y*-value, then the horizontal line that connects them should lie completely inside the polygon. An analogous definition can be made for *vertically convex* polygons. A number of polygons that illustrate these concepts are shown in Figure 9.1.

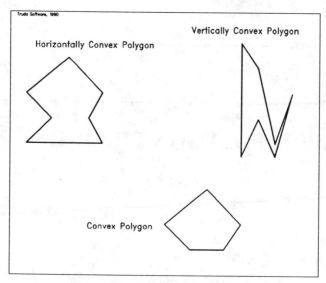

Figure 9.1: Classification of Polygons.

9.2 FLOOD FILLING

One popular algorithm for polygon filling is the flood fill algorithm. It starts out by drawing the outline of the polygon on the screen. The next step is to pick a pixel inside the polygon, set this pixel to the desired color, and then examine all the neighboring pixels. If any of these pixels have the background color, they are also set to the required color. The procedure repeats itself by examining all the neighbors of the new set pixels. When the "flood" of pixels reaches the boundary, the process stops.

Next is an implementation of a subroutine that will flood fill a region, if the outline of the polygon already exists on the screen. The implementation assumes that recursion is available as a language extension to FORTRAN. Some compilers implement recursion, but many don't. It is, however, always possible to change a recursive algorithm into an iterative algorithm by using stacks.

```
      SUBROUTINE FLOOD(X,Y)
C Flood fills a region in the frame buffer.
      INTEGER  X,Y

      ICOL = GETPIX(X,Y)        ! Get the value of pixel at (x,y)
      IF (ICOL .NE. 1) THEN
         CALL SETPIX(X,Y)
         CALL FLOOD(X  ,Y-1)
         CALL FLOOD(X  ,Y+1)
         CALL FLOOD(X-1,Y)
         CALL FLOOD(X+1,Y)
      ENDIF
      RETURN
      END
```

Flood filling is inherently inefficient. This is because the algorithm must on average perform four recursive calls to set a single pixel. In other words, only one out of four calls does any useful work. There are methods, which include the use of stacks, to improve the efficiency of the flood fill algorithm, but they are not discussed in this book.

Flood filling is a valuable method, and will fill any closed shape that is on the screen. It has some disadvantages, however, in that it depends on the shape being on the screen, and it requires a seed pixel in the interior of the shape. It also requires that the screen be free of the fill color. If it is not, the shape may not fill correctly. The first requirement, namely, that the shape of the polygon must be on the screen before filling starts, makes flood filling inappropriate on some output devices. For example, if the output device is a dot-matrix printer and not a graphics display, one cannot test if a pixel (dot) is clear or not.

9.3   A SCAN-LINE ALGORITHM

For these cases a line-by-line approach is needed, and this leads to what is known as *scan-conversion* of the polygon. Simply put, scan-conversion is the process by which a polygon is converted into a series of ordered line segments that are then sent to the output device. Scan-conversion makes no assumptions about initial values on the screen or other output device, and can be used to fill any shape that can be represented as a polygon.

A direct approach to scan-converting a polygon is to determine the maximum as well as minimum scan lines for the polygon. Then start at the maximum scan line and determine which polygon edges are cut by the scan line. The next step is to calculate the x-intercepts of the scan line with these polygon edges, and then draw a horizontal line between the intercepts. The scan line is decremented, and the process is repeated until the minimum scan line is reached. This algorithm is fairly easy to implement, as the next listing shows.

```
      SUBROUTINE POLFIL(X,Y,NV)
C Fills a polygon with "NV" vertices, which are held in arrays
C "X" and "Y". Uses Scan-line Algorithm, but will only fill
C horizontally convex polygons.
      INTEGER      NV ! Number of vertices.
      REAL         X(NV), Y(NV)   ! Arrays that hold vertices.
      REAL         XI,XLIM
      PARAMETER   (XLIM = 1024.0) ! Max. allowable x-coordinate.
      REAL         XMIN, XMAX
      REAL         YMAX, YMIN
      INTEGER      I1,I2,SCAN

C Determine maximum (ymax) and minimum (ymin) scan lines.
      YMAX = Y(1)
      YMIN = Y(1)
      DO 10 I = 2,NV
         YMAX = MAX(YMAX,Y(I))
         YMIN = MIN(YMIN,Y(I))
   10 CONTINUE
```

```
C Scan convert polygon.
      DO 30 SCAN = YMAX,YMIN,-1
         XMIN = XLIM
         XMAX = -1.0
         I1 = NV
         DO 20 I2 = 1,NV
            IF (MAX(Y(I1),Y(I2)) .GE. SCAN .AND.
     +          MIN(Y(I1),Y(I2)) .LE. SCAN .AND.
     +          Y(I1).NE.Y(I2)) THEN
C Calculate x-intercept with current scan line.
               XI=(X(I2)-X(I1))*(SCAN-Y(I1))/(Y(I2)-Y(I1))+X(I1)
               XMIN = MIN(XMIN,XI)
               XMAX = MAX(XMAX,XI)
            ENDIF
            I1 = I2
   20    CONTINUE
         IF (XMIN .LE. XMAX) THEN
            CALL LINE(XMIN,REAL(SCAN),XMAX,REAL(SCAN))
         ENDIF
   30 CONTINUE
      RETURN
      END
```

The subroutine takes three arguments, namely, X,Y, and NV. The arrays X and Y hold the vertices of the polygon, and NV is the number of vertices that the polygon has. First the maximum and minimum scan lines for the polygon are found. Next a DO loop is used to loop over all these scan lines. For each scan line a check is make if any polygon edge intersects the scan line. If it does, the x-coordinate of the intersection is determined. Consider a polygon edge that goes from (x_1,y_1) to (x_2,y_2), and a scan line that intersects that edge at $y = scan$. From elementary geometry if now follows that the x-coordinate of the intersection, or x_i, is given by:

$$x_i = (x_2 - x_1)(scan - y_1)/(y_2 - y_1) + x_1,$$

and the subroutine uses this equation to determine x_i for each scan line. The y-coordinate of the intersection is of course *scan*. When the intersections for each scan line have been calculated, the subroutine calls a routine LINE that does the actual filling in of the pixels.

The reader may have noticed that the arguments to LINE are real and not integer variables. Though this particular algorithm and the algorithm discussed in the next section do not depend on this fact, it does make the implementation of these algorithms somewhat easier.

9.4 GENERAL SCAN-LINE ALGORITHM

The straightforward approach of the previous section to polygon filling has two disadvantages. The first is that it will only fill horizontally concave polygons properly. In many applications this is not a major problem, though, for polygons which are not horizontally concave may be broken up into a number of subpolygons which are. This involves extra processing, however, and this leads to the second disadvantage of the algorithm, namely, it is not very efficient.

It is time consuming to calculate the intersections of each scan line with each polygon edge, but one can speed up this computation markedly. Refer to the next figure, and note that for a given scan line, not all edges are intercepted by that scan line. There is therefore no need to consider all the edges for intersection for each scan line. Edges that are intercepted are called *active edges*, and in many cases the list of active edges stays the same from scan line to scan line. This is called *edge coherence*. To use edge coherence, one needs to maintain a list of all the edges that are cut by the current scan line. This list must be updated on each scan line by possibly deleting edges from or adding edges to the list.

Next, the calculation of the intersections of the current scan line with the active edges can be done on an incremental basis. If a scan line intersects an edge at x_i, and the edge is still active on the next scan line, then the x-coordinate of the next intersection is

$$x_{i+1} = x_i + 1/m$$

where $1/m$ is the inverse of the slope of the edge. Thus, so long as a particular edge is active, intersections with that edge are calculated by simply adding a constant to the previous intersection. This is much faster than computing the intersections from the formula given earlier.

A general polygon fill algorithm makes full use of edge coherence, and will fill any polygon, even those with edges that cut themselves. Before giving a FORTRAN implementation, it is useful to discuss the algorithm in general terms, and to aid in this, consider Figure 9.2. It shows a polygon with six edges that is to be filled. The polygon is "general" — it is not horizontally concave, it cuts itself, and has a horizontal edge. The simple polygon fill algorithm of section 9.3 will not fill this polygon properly.

The general algorithm fills the polygon by performing the following steps for each scan line:

- Determine the x-coordinates of the intersections of the current scan line with all edges
- Sort these edge intersections by increasing x-value
- Group edge intersections in pairs
- Fill pixels on the scan line by drawing horizontal lines between pairs of x-values

Scan line a in the figure at $y = 300.0$ intersects the polygon in four places, namely, at $x = 186.0$, $x = 333.3$, $x = 480.0$, and $x = 572.2$. To fill this scan line, one has to draw a line from $(186.0, 300.0)$ to $(333.3, 300.0)$, and a line from $(300.0, 480.0)$ to $(300.0, 572.2)$. Note that in order to pair intersections, there has to be an even number of intersections.

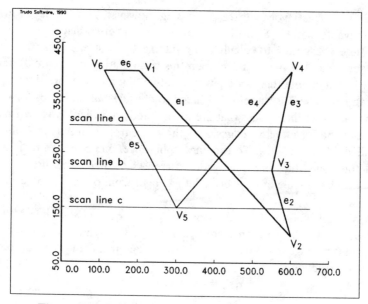

Figure 9.2: Polygon Used to Explain Scan-Line Algorithm.

This is indeed the case for scan line a, but scan line c, however, goes through a vertex, and will result in three intersections, and the algorithm will fail. To solve this problem, one has to count two intersections for the scan line that go through V_5 in the figure. Vertices such V_2, V_4, and V_5 are called local *maxima* or local *minima*, and for these, two intersections are counted. Intersections with other vertices (leaving horizontal ones aside for a moment) count for one intersection. So one would count two intersections at V_2, V_4, and V_5, but only one intersection at V_3. The usual way of ensuring that edge intersections are counted properly is to shorten one of the edges at a vertex which is not a local maxima or minima [42].

The line connecting vertices V_6 and V_1 falls on a scan line, and this special case is handled by deleting the edge from further consideration. To see why this can be done, refer back to the polygon. If the horizontal edge e_6 is deleted from the polygon edge list, it will reappear when the algorithm fills the polygon between edges e_5 and e_1.

9.5 DATA STRUCTURES

To fully exploit edge coherence, a table that contains pertinent information about each edge, called an *edge table*, is constructed. It turns out that four pieces of information about each edge are needed. These are (a) the maximum y-value of the edge, *ymax*, (b) the minimum y-value of the edge, *ymin*, (c) the x-coordinate of the intersection of the current scan line with the edge, and (d) the inverse slope, $1/m$, of the edge. In other languages such as C and Pascal, this information is typically maintained in a *record* or *structure*, and the whole polygon is a list of records. In FORTRAN, parallel arrays will do the job, as shown in Figure 9.3. The figure shows four arrays, YMAX, YMIN, XA, and DA, that hold the information about each edge. YMAX and YMIN hold the maximum y-values of each edge, XA holds the current x-axis value of the intersection of the scan line with the edge, and DA holds the inverse slope of the edge, $1/m$.

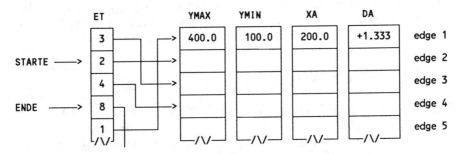

Figure 9.3: Data Structure for Edge Table.

A clear grasp of the edge tables is vital to understanding the algorithm. When the edge table is initially set up, it is sorted on descending *ymax* values, and the *ymax* value of the first edge in the table is the first scan line that needs to be considered; the *ymin*-value of the last entry in the table is the last scan line that must be considered. For each scan line one must determine which edges are active in the edge tables, and for those edges compute the x-intersections, sort and pair the intersections, and then call a line drawing routine to fill in the pixels. The next step is to update the active edges in the edge tables with the new x-intersections and move on to the next scan line.

Note that the algorithm requires that the edge tables be sorted on maximum y-values of each edge when the edge tables are initially constructed, and the active edges must furthermore be sorted on the smallest x-intercept for each scan line. Instead of constantly moving the data in four arrays, it is more efficient to maintain a list of pointers into the edge tables. This is the purpose of the array ET, shown in the Figure 9.3.

The edge tables are best kept as global variables in a COMMON block. Below is an INCLUDE file (called POLY.INC) in which the edge tables are declared, dimensioned, and set up in a COMMON block. This file will be used by selected routines in the polygon fill algorithm.

```
C Include file "POLY.INC" for subroutine POLFIL.
      INTEGER    NP
      PARAMETER  (NP = 50)        ! Max. number of polygon sides
      REAL       YMAX(NP)
      REAL       YMIN(NP)
      REAL       XA(NP)
```

```
      REAL      DX(NP)
      INTEGER   ET(NP)
      INTEGER   IE            ! Number of edges in edge table.
      COMMON    /EDGE/ IE,YMAX,YMIN,XA,DX,ET
```

During filling, only a selected number of edges will be active (i.e., cut by the current scan line) at any one time, so not all the entries in the edge tables need be considered. The variable STARTE points to the first active edge for the current scan line in the edge tables, and the variable ENDE points to the last active edge for the current scan line in table. In the present implementation of the polygon fill algorithm, these two variables are not global, but they might just as well be.

9.6 IMPLEMENTATION

Next is a subroutine POLFIL implemented in FORTRAN. It will fill a polygon with NV vertices, which are held in the arrays X and Y. The implementation of POLFIL closely follows the earlier description of the general polygon fill algorithm. It calls five subroutines, each of which is discussed in following sections.

```
      SUBROUTINE POLFIL(X,Y,NV)
C Fills polygon with "NV" vertices, which
C is held in the arrays "X", and "Y".
      INCLUDE   'POLY.INC'   ! Contains global variables.
      REAL      X(*)
      REAL      Y(*)
      INTEGER   NV
      INTEGER   SCAN          ! Current scan-line.
      INTEGER   STARTE        ! First active edge.
      INTEGER   ENDE          ! Last active edge.

C Check if enough space in COMMON arrays.
      IF (NV.GT.NP) THEN
         WRITE (*,*) 'Error: polygon too large...'
         RETURN
      ENDIF

C Make edge tables, and get "IE", number of edges.
      CALL MKEDGE(X,Y,NV,IE)

C Fill polygon.
      SCAN = YMAX(ET(1))
      ENDE = 1
      STARTE = 1
      CALL INCL(STARTE,ENDE,SCAN)
   10 IF (STARTE.LE.ENDE) THEN
         CALL XSORT(STARTE,ENDE)
         CALL FILL(STARTE,ENDE,SCAN)
         SCAN = SCAN - 1
         CALL UPDATX(STARTE,ENDE)
         CALL INCL(STARTE,ENDE,SCAN)
         GOTO 10
      ENDIF
      RETURN
      END
```

9.7 MAKING THE EDGE TABLES

The first step in the algorithm is building of the polygon edge tables. This is the purpose of the subroutine MKEDGE. It requires two arrays (X and Y) that contain the vertices of the polygon, as well as a variable NV, which is the number of vertices that the polygon has. The subroutine builds the edge tables in three steps. First, it loops over edges and removes horizontal edges from consideration. This means some edges of the polygon are not included in the edge tables, so a counter, IE, is maintained, and this gives the actual number of edges in the edge tables. Edges that are not horizontal are inserted into the edge tables by a call to INSERT, which inserts $ymax$, $ymin$, $1/m$, as well as the initial x-intersection into the edge tables.

Second, MKEDGE calls a subroutine SHORT that shortens the edges that do not form vertices which are local maxima or minima. Finally, MKEDGE calls on a routine YSORT to sort the edges in the edge tables on descending $ymax$-values. The subroutine MKEDGE is listed next.

```
      SUBROUTINE MKEDGE(X,Y,NV,IE)
C Makes edge tables by checking for, and removing
C horizontal edges, shortening (lengthening) vertices
C that are not extrema, then inserting edges in proper
C order into edge tables. Returns the number of entries
C in edge tables as "IE".
      REAL        X(*),Y(*)
      INTEGER     NV,IE
      INTEGER     I1,I2
C
C Loop over all vertices, and insert
C only non-horizontal edges.
      IE = 0
      I1 = NV
      DO 10 I2 = 1,NV
         IF (Y(I1).NE.Y(I2)) THEN
            IE = IE + 1
            CALL INSERT(IE,X(I1),Y(I1),X(I2),Y(I2))
         ENDIF
         I1 = I2
   10 CONTINUE
C
C Shorten edges, and then sort edge tables.
      CALL SHORT()
      CALL YSORT()
      RETURN
      END
```

MKEDGE does not need to know about the edge tables, so it does not use the include file POLY.INC, but the routines INSERT, SHORT, as well as YSORT do, so this file is INCLUDEd in these routines. The subroutine INSERT, listed next, simply inserts the vital information about each edge in the next available location in the edge tables:

```
      SUBROUTINE INSERT(J,X1,Y1,X2,Y2)
C Inserts pertinent information about edge "J",
C with coordinates (X1,Y1), (X2,Y2), into edge tables.
      INCLUDE    'POLY.INC'
      INTEGER    J
      REAL       X1,Y1
      REAL       X2,Y2
C
      YMAX(J) = MAX(Y1,Y2)
      DX(J) = -1.0*(X2-X1)/(Y2-Y1)  ! Insert 1/(slope) of edge.
      IF (Y1.GT.Y2) THEN
         YMIN(J) = Y2
         XA(J)   = X1
      ELSE
         YMIN(J) = Y1
         XA(J)   = X2
      ENDIF
      ET(J) = J    ! Update edge table pointer.
      RETURN
      END
```

In some implementations of the scan-line algorithm, INSERT is combined with an insertion sort algorithm, so that the edge tables are sorted while edges are being added. In the present implementation, however, sorting is a separate step. This is to simplify the implementation of the subroutine that has to shorten edges, namely, SHORT:

```
      SUBROUTINE SHORT()
C Shortens the proper edges in edge tables.
      INCLUDE    'POLY.INC'
      INTEGER    I1,I2
      REAL       Y1,Y2,Y3

C Shorten.
      I1 = IE
      DO 10 I2 = 1,IE
         IF (YMIN(I1).EQ.YMAX(I2)) THEN
            Y1 = YMAX(I1)
            Y2 = YMIN(I1)
            Y3 = YMIN(I2)
            IF (Y1.GT.Y2.AND.Y2.GT.Y3) THEN
               YMIN(I1) = YMIN(I1) + 1     ! Shorten edge.
            ENDIF
         ELSEIF (YMAX(I1).EQ.YMIN(I2)) THEN
            Y1 = YMIN(I1)
            Y2 = YMAX(I1)
            Y3 = YMAX(I2)
            IF (Y1.LT.Y2.AND.Y2.LT.Y3) THEN
               YMIN(I2) = YMIN(I2) + 1     ! Shorten edge.
            ENDIF
         ELSE
            CONTINUE
         ENDIF
         I1 = I2
   10 CONTINUE
      RETURN
      END
```

The third and last stage is to sort the edge tables on descending *ymax*-values. This is performed by YSORT below, which is an implementation of a selection sort algorithm. The edge tables are not sorted directly; rather the index into the tables, ET, is sorted to accomplish the same.

```
      SUBROUTINE YSORT()
C Sorts edge tables according to descending
C ymax-values. Uses a selection sort, and sorts
C by using the index into the edge tables,
C namely, ET.
      INCLUDE    'POLY.INC'
      INTEGER    I,J,M,IT
C
      DO 20 I = 1,IE-1
         M = I
         DO 10 J = I+1,IE
            IF (YMAX(ET(J)) .GE. YMAX(ET(M))) M = J
10       CONTINUE
         IT = ET(M)
         ET(M) = ET(I)
         ET(I) = IT
20    CONTINUE
      RETURN
      END
```

It is a good idea at this point to show what the edge tables for the sample polygon look like just after they have been built by MKEDGE, and this is displayed in Figure 9.4.

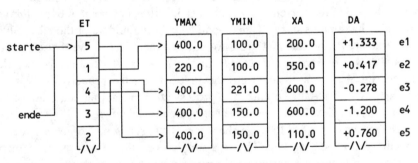

Figure 9.4: Edge Tables for Example Polygon just after Being Built.

9.8 UPDATING THE EDGE TABLE POINTERS

After the edge tables have been built, filling starts at the top-most scan line, which is the *ymax*-value of the entry in the edge tables pointed to by ET(1). In other words, filling starts at scan line *scan* = *ymax(et*(1)). At this stage only one edge (the first) in the edge tables is assumed to be active, so *starte* = *ende* = 1, as shown in Figure 9.4. The subroutine INCL then is called to include any other edges as active edges for this scan line. This subroutine is listed next.

```
      SUBROUTINE INCL(STARTE,ENDE,SCAN)
C Updates the pointers "STARTE", and "ENDE", that delimit
C active edges in ET.
      INCLUDE    'POLY.INC'
      INTEGER    STARTE, ENDE, SCAN
      INTEGER    I, J

C Delete edges if needed.
      DO 20 I = STARTE,ENDE
         IF (SCAN.LT.YMIN(ET(I))) THEN   ! Remove edge.
            DO 10 J = I, STARTE+1,-1
               ET(J) = ET(J-1)            ! Move previous edges down.
   10       CONTINUE
            STARTE = STARTE + 1
         ENDIF
   20 CONTINUE

C Add new edges if needed.
   30 IF (ENDE.LT.IE.AND.SCAN.LE.YMAX(ET(ENDE+1))) THEN
         ENDE = ENDE + 1
         GOTO 30
      ENDIF
      RETURN
      END
```

   INCL starts at the first active edge in the edge tables, and checks all edges down to the last active edge to see if the scan line has not passed the lower end of the edge, namely, *ymin*. If it has, INCL deletes the edge from the list of active edges. Again, the edge table entries are not deleted, but the pointers into the edge tables are manipulated to achieve the same effect. It is easy to delete an edge at the top of the current active edge list, i.e., the edge pointed to by *starte* — one simply increments *starte*. Deleting an edge in the middle of the edge tables is more involved, and one method is to move all the edges above that entry one position down, overwriting that edge in the process. If carefully coded, this method can also be used to delete the first active edge properly. This is the approach used in INCL. To make the process efficient, not all edges above the edge are moved down; only the active edges are moved down.

   In the second part of INCL, a check is make to see if any new edges need to be included for the scan line. This is a simple operation, because the pointers into the edge tables are sorted on descending *ymax*-values, and therefore one just needs to increment *ende* to add a new edge. The reader should note that edges are first deleted and then new ones are added. This cuts down on the number of edges that are considered for deletion, making the subroutine faster.

9.9 SORTING THE *x*-INTERSECTIONS

The next step in the algorithm is to sort all the active edges on ascending *x*-intersections with the current scan line. This task is performed by the routine XSORT, which is shown below. A selection sort is used to sort the entries between *starte* and *ende*, which delimit the active edges in the edge tables.

```
      SUBROUTINE XSORT(STARTE,ENDE)
C Sorts edge tables on ascending x-intersection.
C Uses selection sort, and sorts by using the
C index to the edge, namely,  ET.  Sorts only
C entries between "STARTE", and "ENDE".
      INCLUDE    'POLY.INC'
      INTEGER    STARTE,ENDE
      INTEGER    I
      INTEGER    J
      INTEGER    M
      INTEGER    IT
C
      DO 20 I = STARTE,ENDE-1
         M = I
         DO 10 J = I+1,ENDE
            IF (XA(ET(J)) .LT. XA(ET(M))) M = J
10       CONTINUE
         IT    = ET(M)
         ET(M) = ET(I)
         ET(I) = IT
20    CONTINUE
      RETURN
      END
```

9.10 DRAWING THE LINE SEGMENTS

Following this the intersections are paired and horizontal lines are drawn between coordinate pairs. This is the function of the subroutine FILL, shown below:

```
      SUBROUTINE FILL(STARTE,ENDE,SCAN)
C Fills (draws) line segments for current scan line.
      INTEGER    STARTE, ENDE, SCAN
      INCLUDE    'POLY.INC'
      INTEGER    NX
      INTEGER    J
      INTEGER    K
C
      NX = (ENDE-STARTE+1)/2     ! Number of x-coordinate pairs.
      J = STARTE
      DO 10 K = 1, NX
         CALL LINE(XA(ET(J)),REAL(SCAN),XA(ET(J+1)),REAL(SCAN))
         J = J + 2
10    CONTINUE
      RETURN
      END
```

The variable *scan* is then decremented, and the *x*-intersections of the new scan line with the active edges must be updated. This is done by the routine below, UPDATX. It computes new intersections by adding $1/m$ (kept in DX) for each active edge to the previous *x*-intersection for that edge. This completes one iteration of the complete algorithm, and these steps are repeated until the whole polygon has been filled.

```
      SUBROUTINE UPDATX(STARTE,ENDE)
C Calculates the  x-coordinates of scan line's
C intersections with the polygon edges.
      INCLUDE     'POLY.INC'
      INTEGER     STARTE,ENDE
      INTEGER     I
C
      DO 10 I = STARTE,ENDE
         XA(ET(I)) = XA(ET(I)) + DX(ET(I))
   10 CONTINUE
      RETURN
      END
```

9.11 DISCUSSION

It is clear that this general polygon fill algorithm is much more complicated than the first scan-line algorithm, and it took considerably longer to implement and debug. The algorithm is a good example of incremental computing. Not only are the edge intersections computed on an incremental basis, but the edge tables are also maintained incrementally. The tables are furthermore manipulated (sorted and so on) via a pointer array, and this eliminates a large amount of data transfer. All of this makes for an efficient algorithm.

To measure the exact reduction in execution time that results from using this algorithm is difficult, for many factors play a role. For example, a program that fills many relatively small polygons, with many edges, can benefit substantially from the improved scan-line algorithm. Also, on some hardware, it is quite possible that the time required to set a pixel to a specific color, dominates the execution time to such an extent that all this fancy incremental computing makes only a small difference. Nevertheless, the next table shows the relative execution times of two programs that filled a 5000-polygon scene with both methods, for various compilers:

Compiler	$t_{\text{scan-line}}/t_{\text{simple}}$
Apollo	0.25
Lahey	0.30
VAX	0.33

In the table, $t_{\text{scan-line}}$ is the execution time for the general scan line algorithm, and t_{simple} is the execution time for the first scan line routine, given in Section 9.3. Please note that the values given are only approximate. Other scenes and hardware will likely give substantially different results. Comparing the two algorithms is also in a way similar to comparing apples and oranges, because the general scan-line algorithm can fill polygons that the other one cannot. Still, it should be clear that the general polygon fill algorithm is very efficient.

10

EXAMPLE: FILE COMPRESSION

The need for file compression often arises, especially on mirocomputers. Some of the benefits of file compression are smaller disk space requirements, faster backups, and faster (therefore cheaper) file transfer with modems.

The purpose of the chapter is to describe step by step the implementation of a file compression program, and to show how one goes about optimizing a program. The program will be written in Microsoft FORTRAN, but with the eye on making the program portable. The program is much slower than programs such as PKWARE's PKZIP [43]. It also does not have the multitude of options these commercial programs have. Despite its limitation, it is nevertheless useful, and could easily be transformed into a useful tool.

10.1 HUFFMAN ENCODING

Most files contain a substantial amount of redundant information. It was mentioned in Section 7.6 that one can reduce the size of text file be replacing blanks with tabs. This can be viewed as an elementary form of encoding. Text files contain a lot more redundant information that just spaces, however. Take for example the word queen. In the English language, the letter u always follows the letter q, so one can store queen as qeen in compressed text files. Spaces and u's that follow q's are instances of redundancy in the source, but another aspect of the matter is the way information is stored on disk files.

Normally 8 bits are used to represent characters, which makes it possible to have 256 different characters. If the source file does not use 256, but only, say, 128 characters, only 7 bits are required to store the information. This is a quite common situation, for not many text files contain more that 128 different characters. Storing each character as 7 bits instead of 8 will lead to a 12.5% savings in disk space. Also, not all characters in the file occur with the same frequency, and it follows from information theory that in order to make coding effective, symbols with a high frequency of occurrence should have shorter code words than those that occur seldom in the source. This approach is called *variable length* encoding.

There are several compression algorithms in use, and one of the most popular for text files is the *Huffman algorithm*. While Huffman encoding is optimum for a certain class of coding strategies, it considers characters in the message only on a character-per-character basis, with no regard for the context in which characters are used. Returning to the word *queen*, both *q* and *u* are encoded in Huffman encoding, but from the context it is clear that *u* need not be coded at all. If *u* is not coded, but every occurrence of the letter *q* is replaced with *qu* during decoding, one will decode the word correctly. Thus, Huffman encoding is in general not the most effective coding method. It does, however, make full use of all 8 bits in a byte, and is a variable length code.

The first step in constructing a Huffman code for a message is to determine the frequency of occurrence of each character in the message. All characters must be counted: blanks, spaces, and line feeds. The symbol frequency table is then used to build a *Huffman tree*. This is done by considering each symbol in the frequency table as an *external* node (i.e., a node that has no children) of a tree. Then combine the two nodes with the lowest frequency counts to form a new node. The frequency count for the new node is taken to be the sum of its two children, and the symbol associated with the new node is the combination of the symbols of its children. The process is repeated until all nodes are exhausted.

This is best explained in terms of an example, so consider the message: *this is a test<EOF>*, where *<EOF>*, in an *end-of-file* indicator, which is a single character on MS-DOS systems. The frequency table for this message looks as follows (its peculiar ordering will become clear in later sections):

i	6	7	5	0	2	3	4	1
symbol(i)	s	t	i	EOF	a	e	h	SPACE
freq(i)	3	3	2	1	1	1	1	3

In Figure 10.1 is a Huffman tree for the message. The number to the right of each node is the frequency associated with that node, and it is the sum of the values of its children. The characters to the left of each node is the symbols associated with the particular node. At the outset, several pairs of nodes qualify for nodes with the lowest frequency count. One such pair is nodes *e* and *h*. These two nodes combine to form a new node, *eh*, with frequency count 2.

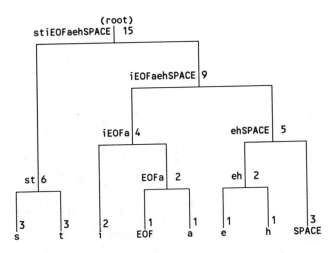

Figure 10.1: Huffman Tree for the Message: *this is a test<EOF>*.

The next pair of nodes is *EOF* and *a*, which combine to form *EOFa* with count 2. Another smallest pair is now *eh* and *SPACE*, and they combine to form node *ehSPACE* with count 5, and so on. The value at the root is the sum of all the external nodes, and is therefore the total number of characters in the message. Since some symbols have the same frequency of occurrence, it is possible to combine nodes differently, so the Huffman tree for a message is seldom unique.

With the Huffman tree for the message in place, characters are encoded by starting at the root of the tree and moving to each of the external nodes. When a left child is selected, then a 1 is associated with that branch. If a right child is selected, then a 0 is associated with the branch. This leads to the encoding tree shown in Figure 10.2, where the numbers in parenthesis is the node number.

For example, to get from the root to the node that holds character *h*, one must select *Right, Right, Left*, and *Right* as one chooses the children at each node. The code for *h* is thus *RRLR*, or 0010. Other codes are derived in a similar fashion. Characters with a high frequency of occurrence, such as *s*, have short codes, and characters with low occurrence, such as *e*, have long codes. This illustrates the fact that the Huffman tree leads to variable length codes, which is what is required for effective compression of files in which some characters occur more frequently that others.

To encode a message, one has to determine the codes for each character in the message and output the codes in sequence. The reader can verify that the complete Huffman code for the message under consideration is:

```
 t   h    i   s    i   s    a    t   e    s   t  <EOF>
10 0010 011 11  000 011 11  000 0100 000 10 0011 11 10 0101
```

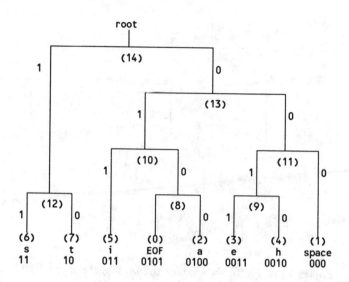

Figure 10.2: Encoding Tree for the Message: *this is a test <EOF>*

When this string of bits are grouped into bytes, the following results:

```
               10001001 11100001 11100001 00000100 01111100 101????
Decimal value    137      225      225        4       124      160
ASCII character   ë        β        β                  |       á
```

The message can therefore be coded into 5 bytes and 3 bits. If one sets the unused bits in the last byte to zero, it follows that the 6 bytes with decimal values 137, 225, 225, 4, 124, and 160 form the Huffman code for the message. With the ASCII representation, which uses one byte per character, the original message will need a total of 15 bytes. This is 2.5 times as much space as the Huffman code for this message. Generally speaking, though, the compression is less dramatic than this example may suggest. Text files are typically compressed to about 45% - 60% of their original size if Huffman coding is used. For example, Huffman encoding of the text for this book compressed the file from about 400KB to roughly 240KB— a 40% savings is disk space.

In summary, then, the steps required for Huffman file compression are the folowing:

- Scan input file and make frequency symbol table
- Use the frequency table to build the Huffman tree
- Write the Huffman tree and associated information to output file
- For each character in the input file, use the Huffman tree and find the bit pattern that corresponds to that character
- Pack the bit patterns into bytes
- Write bytes to output file

To decode the message, one must have the Huffman tree available and also know the location of its root. Then start at the root of the tree, and move left or right depending on the bits in the message. Do this until a node is found that has no children (external node). The symbol at this node is the decoded symbol. Then go back to the root, and repeat the process until all input bits are decoded. For example, the first byte of the coded message is 10001001_2. Starting at the root, the first 1 in the message means one must select the left child, and the following 0 says one must then select a right child. This leads to the external node with symbol t, which is the first character in the message. The other bits in the message are decoded in similar fashion. Next is a summary of the decoding process:

- Read the Huffman tree and its associated information from the compressed file.
- For each character in the compressed file, use the bits in the character to select a right or left child, and do this until a node with no children has been reached.
- The symbol at this node is a decoded character.
- Repeat this process until all characters are decoded.

10.2 DATA STRUCTURES FOR THE HUFFMAN TREE

One must decide at the outset how to represent data in the program. What is required is a way of accessing data on a byte-for-byte basis. On most microcomputer compilers, as well as on the VAX, a single byte is used to represent characters, but in other computing environments this may not be true. Some compilers allow one to declare byte sized variables with an INTEGER*1 specification; others, such as the VAX compilers, have a BYTE data type, which amounts to the same thing. Because the target compiler is the Microsoft compiler, CHARACTER data will be used to hold byte sized variables. This will make the porting the program to other microcomputer FORTRAN compilers, as well as a VAX, easier.

Each node of the Huffman tree will contain five pieces of information as depicted in (a) of Figure 10.3. The first two fields are pointers to the left and right sons of the node, and the third field contains the location of the father of the node. The fourth field holds the symbol associated with the node, and the last field contains the frequency of occurrence of that symbol. In (b) of Figure 10.3 is a section of the Huffman tree for the sample message, *this is a test<EOF>*.

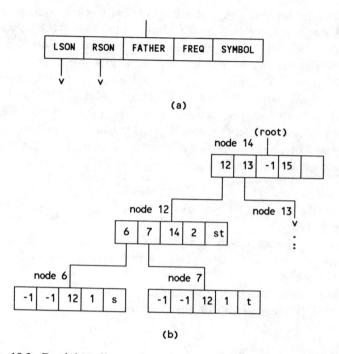

(a)

(b)

Figure 10.3: Partial Huffman Tree for the Message: *this is a test <EOF>*

VAX FORTRAN, as well as version 5 of the Microsoft compiler, supports RECORDs as extensions to the FORTRAN standard, and one possibility is to organize the nodes of the tree as records. Because the aim is to make the program portable, this approach is not followed here. Without a formal RECORD data type, one can still view each node as a record, and implement the RECORDs with parallel arrays, as was done with the polygon fill algorithm, (see Section 9.5):

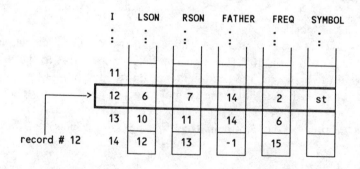

Figure 10.4: Implementing RECORDs with Parallel Arrays.

It can be shown that with n external nodes, the tree will have total of $2*n-1$ nodes. Let *maxsym* designate the maximum allowable number of unique characters or symbols in the input file. Since there is an external node for each unique symbol in the Huffman tree, there will be a maximum of $2*nsym-1$ nodes in the tree, and the arrays can be dimensioned accordingly. To make a Huffman tree for a file that contains the complete ASCII character set, which has 256 different characters, will require $256*2-1 = 511$ entries in each of the arrays.

The Huffman tree is accessed by a number of routines in the file compression program, so the arrays that make up the tree should be global variables. This is done by combining them into a COMMON block, called HTREE. This and some other parameters are put into an include file, called HTREE.INC shown next:

```
C "HTREE.INC", include file for file compression program.
      INTEGER      MAXSYM
      PARAMETER    (MAXSYM = 256)     ! Number of unique symbols.
      INTEGER      MAXNOD
      PARAMETER    (MAXNOD = 2*MAXSYM-1)
      INTEGER      LEFT
      PARAMETER    (LEFT   = 1)
      INTEGER      RIGHT
      PARAMETER    (RIGHT  = 0)
      INTEGER      NONE
      PARAMETER    (NONE   = -1)
C
      INTEGER      NSYM             ! Number of unique symbols in file.
      INTEGER      NC               ! Number of characters in file.
      INTEGER*2    LSON (0:MAXNOD-1)
      INTEGER*2    RSON (0:MAXNOD-1)
      INTEGER*2    FATHER (0:MAXNOD-1)
      INTEGER*4    FREQ (0:MAXNOD-1)
      CHARACTER    SYMBOL (0:MAXSYM-1)
C
      COMMON /HTREE/ NSYM,NC,LSON,RSON,FATHER,FREQ,SYMBOL
```

10.3 I/O ROUTINES

Since all characters in the file, spaces, line feeds, and so on are to be compressed, and later on decompressed, one must find a method for reading and writing bytes without special interpretation to and from disk files. Standard FORTRAN does not allow one to do this, but most compilers support some kind of I/O that is known as *binary* or *transparent* I/O, and this is what is required.

Instead of coding these nonstandard I/O statements at various places into the program, it is best to write a function called FOPEN that opens files, and then call FOPEN each time a file must be opened. This confines the use of the language extension to one subroutine. In (a) below is an implementation of FOPEN for the Microsoft compiler, and in (b) is an include file for the subroutine. The contents of this file will become clear in due course.

```
      SUBROUTINE FOPEN(U,FNAME)
C Opens file "FNAME" as unit "U" in binary/transparent
C mode. For use with Microsoft FORTRAN compiler.
      INCLUDE        'IO.INC'
      INTEGER        U
      CHARACTER*(*)  FNAME
C
      OPEN( UNIT     = U,
     +      FILE     = FNAME,
     +      FORM     = 'BINARY',
     +      BLOCKSIZE = MAXBUF)
      EOF(U) = .FALSE.
      RETURN
      END
```

(a)

```
C Include "IO.INC" file for I/O routines.
      INTEGER     MAXBUF
      PARAMETER   (MAXBUF = 8192)    ! Size of I/O buffers.
      INTEGER     MAXOPEN
      PARAMETER   (MAXOPEN = 2)      ! Maximun # of open files.
      LOGICAL     EOF(MAXOPEN)       ! End of file indicators
C
      COMMON     /IOCMN/ EOF
```

(b)

Routines that close and rewind files are given in (a) and (b) below:

```
      SUBROUTINE FREWIND(U)              SUBROUTINE FCLOSE(U)
      INCLUDE     'IO.INC'               INCLUDE     'IO.INC'
      INTEGER     U                      INTEGER     U
C                                   C
      REWIND(U)                          CLOSE(UNIT=U)
      EOF(U) = .FALSE.                   RETURN
      RETURN                             END
      END
```

         (a)   (b)

In (a) below is the function FGETC that reads one character from a file. In (b) is the subroutine FPUTC that writes a single character to a file. In both instances, it is assumed that the file being read from, or being written to, has been opened in binary mode, typically with FOPEN.

```
      CHARACTER*1 FUNCTION FGETC(U)
C Gets one character (byte) from the file
C connected to unit "U".
      INCLUDE     'IO.INC'
      INTEGER     U
C
      READ(U,END=10,ERR=10)FGETC
      RETURN
10    EOF(U) = .TRUE.
      RETURN
      END
```

(a)

```
      SUBROUTINE FPUTC(U,C)
C Writes a character (byte) "C" to the file
C connected to unit "U".
      INCLUDE    'IO.INC'
      INTEGER    U
      CHARACTER*1  C
C
      WRITE(U)C
      RETURN
      END
```
(b)

Both FGETC and FPUTC use the include file IO.INC, and it contains definitions and declarations common to all I/O routines. The global variable EOF is a LOGIGAL array, each element of which is associated with a file unit number. It is used to indicate whether the end of file has been reached during file I/O. The next program puts some of the file I/O functions through their paces.

```
      PROGRAM     COPY
C Copies file "INPUT" to file "OUTPUT".
      INCLUDE    'IO.INC'
      CHARACTER   FGETC
      CHARACTER   C
      INTEGER     IN,OUT
      PARAMETER   (IN = 1,OUT = 2)
C
      CALL FOPEN(IN,'INPUT')
      CALL FOPEN(OUT,'OUTPUT')

      C = FGETC(IN)
   10 IF (.NOT. EOF(IN)) THEN
          CALL FPUTC(OUT,C)
          C = FGETC(IN)
      GOTO 10
      ENDIF
C
      CALL FCLOSE(IN)
      CALL FCLOSE(OUT)
C
      STOP
      END
```

The program will work fine with the Microsoft compiler, and it is easy to adapt it for use with other compilers. The version of FOPEN given below was written in Lahey FORTRAN, and if it is used instead of the first version of FOPEN, the program COPY will work with this compiler without any other alterations. This is only an simple illustration of the sensibility of containing compiler-dependent features to a few selected routines.

```
      SUBROUTINE FOPEN(U,FNAME)
C Opens file "FNAME" as unit "U" in binary/transparent
C mode. For use with Lahey FORTRAN compiler.
      INCLUDE    'IO.INC'
      INTEGER    U
      CHARACTER*(*)  FNAME
C
```

```
   OPEN( UNIT=U,
+        FILE      =  FNAME,
+        FORM      = 'UNFORMATTED',
+        ACCESS    = 'TRANSPARENT',
+        BLOCKSIZE =  MAXBUF)
   EOF(U) = .FALSE.
   RETURN
   END
```

It also is sound policy from the standpoint of efficiency to keep file I/O operations in a few routines. This is because a program may turn out to be I/O bound, and to improve efficiency one might have to use file buffers and so on. With the I/O operations coded in a large number of routine and files, this can turn out to be a nightmare.

10.4 THE FIRST IMPLEMENTATION

The subroutine ZIP below is the main subroutine that performs the file compression. It takes two arguments: FNAME1, which is the name of the input file, and FNAME2, which is the name to which the compressed file will be written. In addition to the file open and close routines, ZIP calls several other subroutines.

The first is MKTABLE, which creates the frequency and symbol tables for the input file. The next is MKTREE, which creates the Huffman tree from these tables. The file header is then written to the output file by the subroutine MKHEAD, and the subroutine ENCODE then uses the Huffman tree to compress the input file. The files are then closed, and the subroutine returns to its caller.

```
      SUBROUTINE ZIP(FNAME1,FNAME2)
C Uses Huffman encoding to compress file "FNAME1".
C The output is written the file "FNAME2".
      INCLUDE        'HTREE.INC'
      CHARACTER*(*)  FNAME1,FNAME2
      INTEGER        IN
      PARAMETER      (IN = 1)
      INTEGER        OUT
      PARAMETER      (OUT = 2)

C Make symbol tables for file "FNAME1".
      CALL MKTABLE(FNAME1)

C Make Huffman tree.
      CALL MKTREE()

C Write header to file "FNAME2".
      CALL FOPEN(OUT,FNAME2)
      CALL MKHEAD(OUT)

C Compress file.
      CALL FOPEN(IN,FNAME1)
      CALL ENCODE(IN,OUT)
```

```
C Close files and return
      CALL FCLOSE(IN)
      CALL FCLOSE(OUT)
      RETURN
      END
```

In the following sections each of the different subroutines are described in more detail.

10.5 MAKING THE SYMBOL FREQUENCY TABLE

To build the Huffman tree for a file requires a table with all the unique symbols in the file, along with their frequency of occurrence. This is the function of the following subroutine MKTABLE. It is called with the name of the input file, and it then sets the global variable NSYM, which is the number of symbols in the file, as well as the global variable NC, which is the number of characters in the input file. It also stores the symbols, and their frequency counts in the global arrays SYMBOL and FREQ.

The subroutine does its work in four steps. First the frequency tables are cleared. Next the input file is opened, and FGETC is called to read the file character-for-character. Each character is counted, and a count is kept on how many times a specific character has been read. The FORTRAN ICHAR function is used to convert the characters to numeric values, and these are used as indices into the frequency table. Most files will not contain all the 256 different ASCII characters, so the frequency tables will contain a large number of empty spaces.

```
      SUBROUTINE MKTABLE(FNAME)
C Makes symbol and frequency tables.
      INCLUDE        'HTREE.INC'
      INCLUDE        'IO.INC'
      CHARACTER*(*)  FNAME
      INTEGER        I
      INTEGER        J
      INTEGER        INDX
      CHARACTER*1    FGETC
C
C Clear Frequency table.
      DO 10 I = 0,MAXSYM-1
          FREQ(I) = 0
   10 CONTINUE

C Get file size and determine frequency table.
      CALL FOPEN(1,FNAME)
      NC = 0
      INDX = ICHAR(FGETC(1))
   20 IF (.NOT.EOF(1)) THEN
          FREQ(INDX) = FREQ(INDX) + 1
          NC = NC + 1
          INDX = ICHAR(FGETC(1))
      GOTO 20
      ENDIF
      CALL FCLOSE(1)
```

```
C Initialize SYMBOLS table.
      DO 30 I = 0,MAXSYM-1
         IF(FREQ(I) .NE. 0) SYMBOL(I) = CHAR(I)
  30  CONTINUE

C Pack SYMBOLS table.
      I = 0
      DO 40 J = 0,MAXSYM-1
        IF (FREQ(J) .NE. 0) THEN
           FREQ(I)   = FREQ(J)
           SYMBOL(I) = SYMBOL(J)
           IF (I.NE.J) FREQ(J) = 0
           I = I + 1
        ENDIF
  40  CONTINUE
      NSYM = I
C
      RETURN
      END
```

This leads to the third and fourth steps, which are to initialize the symbol table and then pack the frequency and symbol tables, so that they are contiguous in memory. The tables before the packing for the sample message is shown in (a) below, and the packed table in (b).

I	SYMBOL(I)	FREQ(I)
.		
:		
26	EOF	1
.		
:		
32	SPACE	3
.		
:		
97	a	1
.		
:		
101	e	1
.		
:		
104	h	1
105	i	2
.		
:		
115	s	3
116	t	3
.		
:		

(a)

I	SYMBOL(I)	FREQ(I)
0	EOF	1
1	SPACE	3
2	a	1
3	e	1
4	h	1
5	i	2
6	s	3
7	t	3

(b)

10.6 BUILDING THE HUFFMAN TREE

Readers familiar with *heaps* will recognize that by building a minheap out of the frequency table, one will obtain the Huffman tree. Most authors of textbooks follow this approach when discussing building a Huffman tree. See, for example, Sedgewick's [44] book, which also gives Pascal routines which are not to difficult to translate into FORTRAN. Here, however, a direct brute force approach will be followed, simply because is seems the easiest. If it turns out to be inefficient in terms of space or time, other methods will have to be tried. The subroutine that builds the Huffman tree is called MKTREE, and is listed next.

```
        SUBROUTINE MKTREE()
C Builds Huffman tree from frequency tables.
        INCLUDE     'HTREE.INC'
        INTEGER     ROOT
        INTEGER     SMALL1,SMALL2
        INTEGER     I,J
        INTEGER     N1,N2
        INTEGER     M
        INTEGER*4   MAXINT
        PARAMETER   (MAXINT = 2 000 000 000)

C Initialize tree.
        ROOT = (2*NSYM-1) -1
        DO 10 I = 0,ROOT
            FATHER(I) = NONE
            LSON(I)   = NONE
            RSON(I)   = NONE
 10     CONTINUE

C Build tree.
        DO 40 M = NSYM,ROOT
            N1 = 1
            N2 = 1
            SMALL1 = MAXINT
            SMALL2 = MAXINT

C Search for smallest node with no father.
            DO 20 J = 0,M-1
                IF ( FATHER(J).EQ.NONE) THEN
                    IF (FREQ(J).LT.SMALL1.AND.FREQ(J).NE.0) THEN
                        SMALL1 = FREQ(J)
                        N1 = J
                    ENDIF
                ENDIF
 20         CONTINUE

C Search for second most smallest node with no father.
            DO 30 J = 0,M-1
                IF (FATHER(J) .EQ. NONE) THEN
                    IF (FREQ(J).LT.SMALL2.AND.FREQ(J).GE.SMALL1.AND.
     +                  J .NE. N1) THEN
                        SMALL2 = FREQ(J)
                        N2 = J
                    ENDIF
                ENDIF
 30         CONTINUE
```

```
C Found two sons at N1 and N2, now build father node.
          LSON(M)    = N1
          RSON(M)    = N2
          FATHER(N1) = M
          FATHER(N2) = M
          FREQ(M)    = FREQ(N1) + FREQ(N2)
   40  CONTINUE
C
       RETURN
       END
```

The first step is to initialize the nodes. All the father and son nodes are set to NONE, which is defined as -1, in the include file HTREE.INC. There are *nsym* terminal nodes, and from the properties of binary trees it follows that there are a total of 2*nsym-1 nodes, so there are *nsym*-1 father nodes to build. The subroutine does this by looping over these nodes, and on each iteration finds the two sons that have the smallest frequency counts. The smallest of these two becomes the left son of the new father node, and the other becomes the right son.

The frequency counts of the sons are added, and this becomes the frequency count for the new father node. This node now becomes a potential son for future father nodes. The whole process is repeated until the root node is reached. Note that when the tree is built, the terminal nodes all have sons NONE, and the root node has father NONE.

Next is the contents of the arrays that make up the Huffman tree for the sample message. Note that while the Huffman tree in Section 10.1 shows the symbols at nodes other than the terminal nodes, only the symbols at the terminal nodes are necessary for encoding, so they are the only ones maintained in the array SYMBOL.

```
************************************************
 NODE  SYMBOL(I) FREQ(I) FATHER(I) LSON(I) RSON(I)
************************************************
   0     EOF       1        8       -1      -1
   1     SPACE     3       11       -1      -1
   2     a         1        8       -1      -1
   3     e         1        9       -1      -1
   4     h         1        9       -1      -1
   5     i         2       10       -1      -1
   6     s         3       12       -1      -1
   7     t         3       12       -1      -1
   --------------------------------------------
   8               2       10        0       2
   9               2       11        3       4
  10               4       13        5       8
  11               5       13        9       1
  12               6       14        6       7
  13               9       14       10      11
  14              15       -1       12      13
```

Note: -1 = "NONE"

10.7 WRITING THE FILE HEADER

Several bits of information are written as a file header to the output file, and these include the number of characters NC in the original file, NSYM, the number of unique symbols in the original file, the arrays LSON, RSON, and SYMBOL which contains the Huffman tree, as well as ROOT, the location of the root node in the Huffman tree. All this information is needed by the program that will decode the compressed file.

In addition to this, three *identification bytes* are written to the output file. These bytes are, strictly speaking, not needed, but they offer the user of the decompression program some protection. The first of the three bytes is the arbitrarily chosen character CHAR(8). The second is a version number, and since this is the first of the Huffman compression program, CHAR(1) is written to the file. The last byte contains a code that indicates what kind of compression was applied to the file, and CHAR(1) is used to signify Huffman encoding.

```
      SUBROUTINE MKHEAD(U)
c Write the file header to file connected to unit "U".
      INCLUDE      'HTREE.INC'
      INTEGER      U,I,ROOT

C Write special ID characters.
      WRITE(U)CHAR(8)    ! ID Byte.
      WRITE(U)CHAR(1)    ! Version 1.0 of compression program.
      WRITE(U)CHAR(1)    ! => Huffman encoding.

C Write rest of header.
      ROOT = (2*NSYM - 1) - 1
      WRITE(U)NC,ROOT
      WRITE(U)(LSON(I),I=0,ROOT)
      WRITE(U)(RSON(I),I=0,ROOT)
      WRITE(U)NSYM
      WRITE(U)(SYMBOL(I),I=0,NSYM-1)
      RETURN
      END
```

A decompression program should check these three bytes before attempting to decode a file, for the system may very well crash if an uncompressed file is used as input. It is of course still likely that some (uncompressed) file might have the "proper" identification bytes, so the system is not foolproof. On the other hand, the alternative is no protection at all.

10.8 GENERATING THE HUFFMAN CODES

With the Huffman tree in place, compression is performed as follows. For each character in the input file, determine which terminal node corresponds to that symbol. Then start at that node, and if it is a right son of its father generate a 1 bit, otherwise generate a 0 bit. Then move on to the father, and repeat the process until the root is reached. The stream of bits that results from this procedure is the desired Huffman code. The subroutine ENCODE listed next will perform these steps. It calls on two other subroutines, LSEARCH and PACK. The purpose of the latter is to pack (or group) the Huffman codes of the characters into bytes and then write these bytes to the output file. PACK will be discussed in more detail in the next section.

```
      SUBROUTINE ENCODE(IN,OUT)
C Encodes file associated with file unit "IN", and write
C output to file unit "OUT".  Uses Huffman tree for encoding.
      INCLUDE      'HTREE.INC'
      INTEGER      IN,OUT
      INTEGER      I,K,IB,BITS
      CHARACTER    FGETC,C
      INTEGER      IBSET
      EXTERNAL     IBSET
C
      DO 20 K = 1,NC
         C = FGETC(IN)
         CALL LSEARCH(C,SYMBOL,NSYM,I)
         BITS = 0
         IB   = 0
10       IF (FATHER(I) .NE. NONE) THEN
            IF (I.EQ.LSON(FATHER(I))) BITS = IBSET(BITS,IB)
            IB = IB + 1
            I = FATHER(I)
         GOTO 10
         ENDIF
         IB = IB - 1
         CALL PACK(IB,BITS,OUT)
20    CONTINUE

C Flush last byte, and return.
      BITS = 0
      CALL PACK(15,BITS,OUT)
      RETURN
      END
```

Because the stream of bits that the Huffman encoding produces seldom makes up an integral number of bytes, it is very likely that a few bits in the very last byte of the Huffman code remain unused. One must ensure that all the bits in the Huffman code are written to the output file, and this is accomplished with the two statements:

```
      :
      :
      BITS = 0
      CALL PACK(15,BITS,OUT)
      :
      :
```

This instructs PACK to pack, and then write a "code," of which all bits are cleared, to the output file. There are 16 bits in the code (remember: numbering of the bits starts at 0), so this will ensure that, apart from flushing the last byte, a byte with all its bits cleared is written to the encoded file. If it so happens that the total number of bits in the Huffman code makes up an integral number of bytes, *two* of these bytes are output. In any event, the very last byte in the compressed file has all of its bits set to zero.

The other subroutine that ENCODE calls is the subroutine LSEARCH, and it performs a linear search for the position of character C in the table TABLE:

```
      SUBROUTINE LSEARCH(C,TABLE,N,INDX)
C Returns index ("INDX") of "C" in "TABLE". A linear
C search isperformed, and "C" MUST be in the table,
C otherwise wrong index will be returned.
      INTEGER    N,INDX
      CHARACTER  TABLE(0:N-1),C
C
      DO 10 INDX = 0,N-1
         IF (C .EQ. TABLE(INDX)) RETURN
 10   CONTINUE
      RETURN
      END
```

A linear search is used at this point, mainly because it is so easy to implement.

10.9 PACKING THE CODE BITS

Each character in the input file results in an unique code, which in general is not 8 bits long. The codes must be grouped into bytes before being written to the output file. The subroutine PACK below performs this function. It takes three arguments, an unit number U, which is the output file unit, an integer variable BITS that holds the code bits, and, finally, an integer variable IB that indicates the length of the bit pattern in BITS. For example, if the code is the bit pattern 100, then BITS is 100_2 = 4 and IB = 2. Note that IB is 2, and not 3, because the bits are numbered as 0, 1, ..., 7 in each byte.

```
      SUBROUTINE PACK(IB,BITS,U)
      INTEGER    U,IP,K,IB
      INTEGER    BITS,IC,IBSET
      LOGICAL    BTEST
      EXTERNAL   IBSET,BTEST
      SAVE       IP,IC
      DATA       IP,IC  /7,0/

      DO 10 K = IB,0,-1
         IF (BTEST(BITS,K)) IC = IBSET(IC,IP)
         IP = IP - 1
         IF (IP .LT. 0) THEN
            CALL  FPUTC(U,CHAR(IC))
            IC = 0        ! Clear bits in "IC"
            IP = 7
         ENDIF
 10   CONTINUE
      RETURN
      END
```

The operation of PACK is quite straightforward. It starts at the leftmost bit of the code bit (at position IB) in BITS, and tests each bit. If the bit is set, a corresponding bit in an integer variable IC is set. The variable IP points to the next open bit position in IC and is decremented in each iteration of the loop. At any time when IP becomes less than 0, it means that IC contains 8 bits, so it is written to the output file with FPUTC. Next all the bits in IC are cleared, IP is reset to point to the leftmost bit in IC, and the rest of BITS is scanned for set bits.

The logical function BTEST used in this subroutine tests if a specific bit in one of its arguments are set, and the function IBSET is used to set bits. Since many compilers implement these functions as intrinsic functions, they are declared as EXTERNAL functions at this stage. This will force the compiler to employ user-written versions of these functions. The implementation of these two routines is described next.

10.10 IMPLEMENTATION OF BTEST AND IBSET

It was shown earlier (in Section 8.3) that if the statement MOD(N,2) is not zero, then N is odd or, in other words, the bit in position 0 is set. This idea is used to test if any bit in a variable is set. First the bit pattern is shifted to the right, so that the bit that must be tested for is in position 0. The resulting number is then tested to see if it is odd. If it is odd, the bit is set. The listing below implements these ideas. Bit shifting is done by division with the proper power of 2.

```
      LOGICAL FUNCTION  BTEST(WORD,BIT)
C Returns .TRUE. if "BIT" is set in "WORD".
      INTEGER   WORD,BIT
      INTEGER   I

      I = 2**BIT
      IF (MOD(WORD/I,2).NE.0) THEN
         BTEST = .TRUE.
      ELSE
         BTEST = .FALSE.
      ENDIF
      RETURN
      END
```

Setting a bit in a variable is accomplished by adding the proper power of 2 to the variable, but only if the bit is not already set. Thus, one has to test each bit before setting it:

```
      INTEGER FUNCTION IBSET(WORD,BIT)
C Sets "BIT" in "WORD".
      INTEGER   WORD,BIT
      INTEGER   I

      I = 2**(BIT)
      IF (MOD(WORD/I,2) .NE. 0) THEN
         IBSET = WORD
      ELSE
         IBSET = WORD + I
      ENDIF
      RETURN
      END
```

10.11   A PROFILE OF THE PROGRAM

This completes the first implementation of the Huffman compression program, and this is a good place to give a subroutine tree of the file compression program:

```
        ZIP
            FOPEN
            FCLOSE
            MKTABLE
                    FOPEN
                    FCLOSE
                    FGETC
            MKTREE
            MKHEAD
            ENCODE
                    FGETC
                    PACK
                        FPUTC
                        BTEST
                        IBSET
```

The Microsoft compiler does not have a profiler available, but because the program is implemented on a modular basis, it is not very difficult to get a rough profile by inserting calls to a timing routine at a few selected places in the code. To measure the execution speed, a 25,000-byte text file, consisting of FORTRAN programs from this book, was used as input, and the compression time was measured. Measurements were made on an AT clone, with a 20 msec hard disk, and a quick measurement of the routines shows that about 11% of the time is spent in the subroutine MKTREE, about 88% of the time is spent in the subroutine ENCODE, and the other 1% is taken up by MKHEAD and the subroutine that builds the Huffman tree, namely, MKTREE.

It immediately shows that the decision to build the tree with a brute force approach, instead of the more elegant methods that use minheaps and so forth, was the correct one. It is uncomplicated and fast. Because most of the time is spent in ENCODE, it was profiled next. The listing below shows how this was done:

```
       SUBROUTINE ENCODE(IN,OUT)
              .
              :
       TFGETC = 0.0
       TLS    = 0.0
       TCODE  = 0.0
       TPACK  = 0.0

       DO 20 K = 1,NC
          CALL TIMER(T1)
          C = FGETC(IN)
          CALL TIMER(T2)
          TFGETC = TFGETC + (T2 - T1)
          CALL TIMER(T1)
          CALL LSEARCH(C,SYMBOL,NSYM,I)
          CALL TIMER(T2)
          TLS = TLS + (T2 - T1)
          BITS = 0
          IB   = 0
 10       CONTINUE
          CALL TIMER(T1)
          IF (FATHER(I) .NE. NONE) THEN
             IF (I.EQ.LSON(FATHER(I))) BITS = IBSET(BITS,IB)
             IB = IB + 1
             I = FATHER(I)
          GOTO 10
          ENDIF
          CALL TIMER(T2)
          TCODE = TCODE + (T2 -T1)
              .
              :
       TTOT = TFGETC+TLS+TCODE+TPACK
       WRITE(*,1)'TTOT   = ',TTOT  ,' = ',100.0,'%'
       WRITE(*,1)'TFGETC = ',FTGETC,' = ',(100.0*TFGETC)/TTOT,'%'
       WRITE(*,1)'TLS    = ',TLS   ,' = ',(100.0*TLS)/TTOT   ,'%'
       WRITE(*,1)'TCODE  = ',TCODE ,' = ',(100.0*TCODE)/TTOT ,'%'
       WRITE(*,1)'TPACK  = ',TPACK ,' = ',(100.0*TPACK)/TTOT ,'%'
 1     FORMAT(1X,A,F15.3,A,F15.3,A)
       RETURN
       END
```

Calls to a timing routine TIMER were placed before and after each invocation of the subroutines that ENCODE calls. The measured time difference was then added to a variable that keeps track of the total time spend by that subroutine. For example, the fragment

```
              :
       CALL TIMER(T1)
       C = FGETC(IN)
       CALL TIMER(T2)
       TFGETC = TFGETC + (T2 - T1)
              :
```

accumulates the time spent executing FGETC in the variable TFGETC. At the end of the subroutine, these times are converted to and then printed as percentages of the total time spent inside the subroutine. Four measurements were made for ENCODE, three of which are for the subroutines FGETC, LSEARCH, and PACK. The other measurement was for the piece of code that walks through the Huffman tree to find the Huffman codes for the input characters. These measurements show that inside ENCODE, 22% of the time is taken up by FGETC, 11% by LSEARCH, 46% by PACK, and 21% by the part that finds the Huffman code.

Inside ENCODE, the subroutine PACK is the most expensive, and to profile it the same approach is used, but with a slight variation. This is shown below:

```
SUBROUTINE PACK(IB,BITS,U)
INTEGER     U              ! File unit.
INTEGER     IP,K,IB
INTEGER     BITS
INTEGER     IC
INTEGER     IBSET
LOGICAL     BTEST
EXTERNAL    IBSET,BTEST
COMMON      /TIME/ TFPUTC,TBITS   ! Define COMMON Block.
SAVE        IP,IC
DATA        IP,IC  /7,0/

DO 10 K = IB,0,-1
   call timer(t1)
   IF (BTEST(BITS,K)) IC = IBSET(IC,IP)
   call timer(t2)
   tbits = tbits + (t2-t1)
   IP = IP - 1
   IF (IP .LT. 0) THEN
       call timer(t1)
       CALL FPUTC(U,CHAR(IC))
       call timer(t2)
       tfputc = tfputc + (t2-t1)
       IC = 0          ! Clear bits in "IC"
       IP = 7
   ENDIF
10 CONTINUE
RETURN
END
```

A COMMON block is defined, which contains the timing variables TFPUTC and TBITS. These variables are repeatedly updated inside PACK, and then just before the program terminates, one can access their values to determine how much time was spent where in PACK. Note that TBITS is the combined execution time for the bit-manipulation functions BTEST and IBSET, and it turns out that these two take up about 86% of the execution time inside PACK.

This completes the examination of ENCODE and the subroutines called by it. The other subroutine that takes up a substantial portion of the compression program's execution time is MKTABLE, and it was also measured. One section of code that calls FGETC accounts for just about all the time inside this routine.

The next tree summarizes the measurements made. It is an edited version of the subroutine tree given earlier. The number at each subroutine is time the routine takes as a fraction of the execution time of its parent. From this tree one can create a profile of the routines in the program.

ZIP

MKTABLE - 0.11

FGETC - 1.0

ENCODE - 0.88

FGETC - 0.22

LSEARCH - 0.11

"CODE' - 0.21

PACK - 0.46

FPUTC - 0.14

BTEST, IBSET - 0.86

For example, references to FGETC inside ENCODE account for 22% of ENCODE's execution time, which in turn is 88% of the total execution time. Thus, the contribution of FGETC inside ENCODE is 0.88 x 0.22 = 19.4% of the total time. Similarly, FGETC accounts for 11% of the total time through its use in MKTABLE, so for the whole program, FGETC is responsible for 30.4% of the execution time.

If the same is done for the other routines, the next profile results:

```
Total running time: 39.40 sec

Routine        cum %   %    sec

IBSET, BTEST   34.8   34.8  13.7   ********************
FGETC          65.2   30.4  12.0   ******************
"CODE"         83.7   18.5   7.3   **********
LSEARCH        93.4    9.7   3.8   *****
FPUTC          99.1    5.7   2.3   ***
```

where "CODE" refers to the section of code in ENCODE that gets the Huffman codes for each character from the Huffman tree.

10.12   OPTIMIZATION: BTEST AND IBSET

Most of the time is spent in the two bit-manipulation functions, BTEST and IBSET, so these are the first target for optimization. These two functions are used many times. For the 25,000-byte test file, for example, BTEST is called 111,689 times, and IBSET is called 99,914 times. Instead of implementing them as functions, they might also be coded directly into the subroutines that use them, e.g., PACK:

```
      SUBROUTINE PACK(IB,BITS,U)
      INTEGER    U              ! File unit.
      INTEGER    IP,K,IB
      INTEGER    BITS
      INTEGER    IC,M,N
      SAVE       IP,IC,M
      DATA       IP,IC,M   /7,0,128/
C
      N = 2**IB
      DO 10 K = IB,0,-1
      IF (MOD(BITS/N,2).NE.0) IC = IC+M
         M = M/2
         N = N/2
         IP = IP - 1
         IF (IP .LT. 0) THEN
            CALL FPUTC(U,CHAR(IC))
            IC = 0
            IP = 7
            M = 128
         ENDIF
  10  CONTINUE
      RETURN
      END
```

This will remove a total of 211,603 function calls and also update the variable IC incrementally. The combined effect of this is significant, and the execution time was reduced by 4.5 sec, or by about 12%. The down side is that PACK is not as clear as the original implementation, and it will take most people a little while to figure out that the fragment

```
         .
         :
      N = 2**IB
      DO 10 K = IB,0,-1
      IF (MOD(BITS/N,2).NE.0) IC = IC+M
         IP = IP - 1
         M = M/2
         .
         :
```

tests whether a bit in BITS is set and, depending on the outcome, sets a bit in the variable IC. Thus the logic of the code is obscured by the optimization, but the code is still as portable as the first version. On the other hand, the bit-manipulation functions, obscured as they are as a result of the inline coding in this implementation of PACK, are still a major bottleneck in the program.

Another appoach is to sacrifice some portability and use Microsoft FORTRAN's intrinsic bit-manipulation functions. The BTEST and IBSET functions (as well as some others) are available on many compilers, so it will not cause too many porting problems if they are used. To use the intrinsic versions of BTEST and IBSET, one has only to remove the EXTERNAL delarations of the functions where they occur in the source code. By using ther bit-manipulation functions, one will restore the readability of PACK and improve execution speed substantially. In fact, with the intrinsic versions of BTEST and IBSET, total execution time dropped to 26 sec, or to 66% of the initial value.

10.13 OPTIMIZATION: BUFFERED I/O

An updated program profile can now be found by accounting for the reduced execution time of BTEST and IBSET. (Note that no new measurements are needed.) This is displayed below. At this point the program is clearly I/O bound, and about 45% of its time is spent reading characters from the disk file. The next optimization step, then, is to write some file I/O routines that will reduce this time.

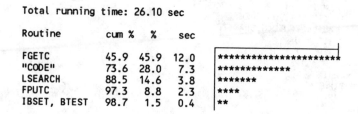

```
Total running time: 26.10 sec

Routine        cum %   %    sec

FGETC          45.9   45.9  12.0   ***********************
"CODE"         73.6   28.0  7.3    **************
LSEARCH        88.5   14.6  3.8    *******
FPUTC          97.3    8.8  2.3    ****
IBSET, BTEST   98.7    1.5  0.4    **
```

The design of the subroutines discussed next were loosely based on those of Jones and Crabtree [45] , but specifically tailored for the file compression program. In any event, they are not meant to be the last word on I/O routines. The basic idea is to maintain a set of I/O buffers together with their buffer pointers. Figure 10.5 shows this organization, where the buffers are implemented with an array of character strings, and the list of buffer pointers are kept in an array of integers, BP. The variable U is the unit number assoiated with the buffer. Also shown is the EOF array that can be used to keep track of when the end of a file has been reached. As an example of how the file system works, the character at BUFFER(BP(U))(3:3)) with U = 2 is BUFFER(2)(3:3), which is "i" in Figure 10.5.

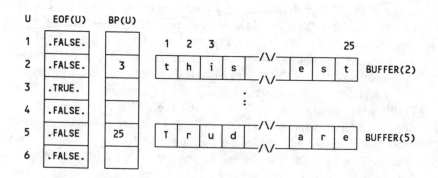

Figure 10.5: Schematic of I/O Buffer System.

The I/O buffers will be accessed by a number of routines, so they are global variables and are kept in a COMMON block in the file IO.INC:

```
C
C Include file for I/O routines.
C
      INTEGER     MAXBUF
      PARAMETER   (MAXBUF = 8192)           ! Size of I/O buffers.
      INTEGER     MAXOPEN
      PARAMETER   (MAXOPEN = 2)             ! Maximum # of open buffers
      CHARACTER   BUFFER*(MAXBUF)(MAXOPEN)
      INTEGER     BP(MAXOPEN)               ! Pointers to I/O buffers.
      LOGICAL     EOF(MAXOPEN)              ! End of file indicators
      COMMON      /IOCMN/ BP,EOF,BUFFER
```

Note that character strings, and not arrays of character variables, are used as buffers. This is because operations on character strings often compile into much more efficient code compared to what equivalent operations on character arrays compile into. Initially, when a file U is opened, BP(U), which is the buffer pointer of file unit U, is set to zero:

```
      SUBROUTINE FOPEN(U,FNAME)
      INCLUDE       'IO.INC'
      INTEGER       U
      CHARACTER*(*) FNAME
C
      OPEN( UNIT      = U,
     +      FILE      = FNAME,
     +      FORM      = 'BINARY',
     +      BLOCKSIZE = MAXBUF)
      BP(U) = 0
      EOF(U) = .FALSE.
      RETURN
      END
```

The file buffers are not accessed directly, but through the routines FGETC and FPUTC. The very first time FGETC is used to read a character after a file has been opened, the buffer must be filled. Once the buffer is full, FGETC gets a character from the buffer and then increments BP(U). When the end of the buffer, indicated by the constant MAXBUF, is reached, the buffer must be filled again:

```
      CHARACTER*1 FUNCTION FGETC(U)
C Gets one byte from file connected to unit "U".
      INCLUDE    'IO.INC'
      INTEGER    U
C
      IF (BP(U) .GT. MAXBUF .OR. BP(U) .EQ. 0) THEN
         READ(U,ERR=10)BUFFER(U)(1:MAXBUF)
10       CONTINUE                 ! Ignore errors
         BP(U) = 1
      ENDIF
      FGETC = BUFFER(U)(BP(U):BP(U))
      BP(U) = BP(U) + 1
C
      RETURN
      END
```

Note that this implementation of FGETC does not set the array EOF when the end of the file has been reached, and it ignores file errors. To understand why, consider the next fragment, taken from subroutine MTABLE (see Section 10.5). This code does two things, namely, it builds the frequency table FREQ, and at the same time counts the number of characters, NC, in the input file.

```
            :
            :
C Get file size and determine frequency table.
      CALL FOPEN(1,FNAME)
      NC = 0                         ! Number of characters in input file.
      INDX = ICHAR(FGETC(1))
   20 IF (.NOT.EOF(1)) THEN
         FREQ(INDX) = FREQ(INDX) + 1
         NC = NC + 1
         INDX = ICHAR(FGETC(1))
      GOTO 20
      ENDIF
      CALL FCLOSE(1)
            :
            :
```

To do this, one must check for an EOF condition each time a character is read. Alternatively, one can determine the number of characters with a separate routine, say, FSIZE, and then use a DO loop to read in the exact number of characters. A version of MTABLE implemented this way is shown below:

```
      SUBROUTINE MKTABLE(FNAME)
C Makes symbol and frequency tables.
      INCLUDE          'HTREE.INC'
      INCLUDE          'IO.INC'
      CHARACTER*(*)    FNAME
      INTEGER          I
      INTEGER          J
      INTEGER          INDX
      CHARACTER*1      FGETC

C Clear Frequency table.
      DO 10 I = 0,MAXSYM-1
         FREQ(I) = 0
   10 CONTINUE

C Get file size...
      CALL FSIZE(FNAME,NC)

C Now determine frequency table.
      CALL FOPEN(1,FNAME)
      DO 20 I = 1,NC
         INDX = ICHAR(FGETC(1))
         FREQ(INDX) = FREQ(INDX) + 1
   20 CONTINUE
      CALL FCLOSE(1)

C Initialize SYMBOLS table.
      DO 30 I = 0,MAXSYM-1
         IF(FREQ(I) .NE. 0) SYMBOL(I) = CHAR(I)
   30 CONTINUE
```

```
C Pack SYMBOLS table.
      I = 0
      DO 40 J = 0,MAXSYM-1
         IF (FREQ(J) .NE. 0) THEN
            FREQ(I)   = FREQ(J)
            SYMBOL(I) = SYMBOL(J)
            IF (I.NE.J) FREQ(J)   = 0
            I = I + 1
         ENDIF
   40 CONTINUE
      NSYM = I
C
      RETURN
      END
```

With this technique, FGETC can be implemented somewhat simpler (and faster) than an implementation that accounts for end-of-file conditions would be. The main advantage in determining the file size separately, however, comes with later optimization, for this is typically a routine that one might want to replace with a call to the operating system, which will often be able to rapidly determine the file size.

The subroutine FSIZE is readily implemented in FORTRAN, however, as the next listing shows. The basic idea is to read data from the file until the end of the file is reached. By keeping track of the number of bytes read, one will determine the file size. Because it is more efficient to read blocks of data (see Chapter 7) than single bytes, it is more efficient to first get a rough estimate of the size of the file by reading large blocks of bytes from the file into a dummy buffer until an end-of-file condition occurs. At this stage the size of the file is known to within the size of one of these "chunks."

```
      SUBROUTINE  FSIZE(FNAME,SIZE)
C Determines the size (in bytes) of "FNAME".
      CHARACTER*(*)  FNAME
      INTEGER        SIZE
      INTEGER        I,J
      INTEGER        IERR
      INTEGER        BUFSZE
      PARAMETER      (BUFSZE = 4096)
      CHARACTER      BUFFER*(BUFSZE)
      DATA           IERR,J   /0,0/

c Determine size to within "BUFSZE" bytes.
      CALL FOPEN(1,FNAME)
   10 IF (IERR .EQ. 0) THEN
          READ(1,IOSTAT=IERR)BUFFER
          J = J + 1
      GOTO 10
      ENDIF
      SIZE = (J-1)*BUFSZE

C Perform a byte sized search from now on.
      CALL FREWIND(1)
      IERR = 0
      DO 20 I = 1,J-1
          READ(1)BUFFER
   20 CONTINUE
```

```
 30   IF (IERR .EQ. 0) THEN
          READ(1,IOSTAT=IERR)BUFFER(1:1)
          SIZE = SIZE + 1
      GOTO 30
      ENDIF
      SIZE = SIZE - 1
      CALL FCLOSE(1)
      RETURN
      END
```

The file is then rewound, and the process is repeated, but stopped just before the end-of-file condition is reached. Then single bytes are read until the end of the file is reached and the size of the file is known. The best size of the dummy buffer used in the rough estimate phase depends on the size of the files being measured. If the buffer is too large, say larger that the file, then FSIZE will end up reading the whole file byte-for-byte anyway. If the buffer is too small, then the program will spend too much time making a rough estimate of the file size.

Output to a file is the task of FPUTC, which is given in (a) below. It does this by placing the character C at the proper position in the buffer associated with file unit U. A check is then made to see if the end of the buffer has been reached, in which case the routine FLUSH is called, which actually writes the data to the disk file. FLUSH is listed in (b).

```
      SUBROUTINE FPUTC(U,C)
C Writes a character (byte) "C" to the
C file connected to unit "U".
      INCLUDE    'IO.INC'
      INTEGER    U
      CHARACTER*1  C
C
      BP(U) = BP(U) + 1
      BUFFER(U)(BP(U):BP(U)) = C
      IF (BP(U) .EQ. MAXBUF) CALL FLUSH(U)
      RETURN
      END
```

                                        (a)


```
      SUBROUTINE FLUSH(U)
      INCLUDE    'IO.INC'
C Writes contents of file "U" to disk.
      INTEGER    U
C
      WRITE(U)BUFFER(U)(1:BP(U))
      BP(U) = 0
      EOF(U) = .FALSE.
      RETURN
      END
```
                                        (b)

The other file I/O routines, FREWIND and FCLOSE, are essentially the same as the previous implementations, except that the buffer pointers are updated when the routines are called:

```
      SUBROUTINE FREWIND(U)              SUBROUTINE FCLOSE(U)
      INCLUDE   'IO.INC'                 INCLUDE   'IO.INC'
      INTEGER   U                        INTEGER   U
C                                    C
      REWIND(U)                          CLOSE(UNIT=U)
      BP(U) = 0                          BP(U) = 0
      EOF(U) = .FALSE.                   RETURN
      RETURN                             END
      END
                (a)                                  (b)
```

Why this somewhat elaborate arrangement just to mainatain two files, one for the input and one for the output? Well, it allows for easy experimentation with buffer sizes. Next, it allows for easy expansion of the file system, just by altering a few constants in the include file. Finally, as in the case of the original file routines, any "funny stuff" is localized to a few routines.

The size of the I/O file buffers determines the effectiveness of buffered I/O. This is supported by the following table, which also shows that the optimum buffer size is about 8192 bytes. With the buffers this size, the total program execution time is reduced from from 26.1 sec to 14.5 sec.

Buffer Size	$t_{execution}$
2048	16.2
4096	15.5
8192	**14.5**
16384	14.9

10.14 OPTIMIZATION: LOOK-UP TABLES

If one accounts for the reduced execution time, which came mainly from more efficient operation of FGETC, the execution profile looks something like this:

```
Total running time: 14.50 sec

Routine         cum %   %    sec

"CODE"          50.0    50   7.3   |**********************
LSEARCH         77.0    26   3.8   |***********
FPUTC           92.0    16   2.3   |****
IBSET, BTEST    94.7    2.7  0.4   |**
FGETC           97.4    2.7  0.4   |**
```

Presently, the subroutine ENCODE encodes each symbol in the input file by starting at the symbol's node, and then moves to the root of the tree, collecting set (1) or cleared (0) bits on the way. This is not very efficient, because the same procedure is repeated many times over. The program section in ENCODE that does this was referred to as "CODE," and at this stage it takes up about 50% of the execution time. Note that the number of different codes are small, not more that 256. It therefore makes sense to create a table that holds the codes before encoding starts. During encoding, a symbol's code is then looked up instead of being redetermined.

To accomplish this, define a two-dimensional array, called CODES, and let CODES(1,I) hold the code for symbol I and CODES(2,I) hold the length of the code for symbol I. The next subroutine, MKCODES, will then initialize this array:

```
      SUBROUTINE MKCODES(CODES)
C Generates lookup tables for compression codes.
      INCLUDE         'HTREE.INC'
      INTEGER         CODES(2,0:MAXNOD-1)
      INTEGER         BITS,IB
      INTEGER         I,J
      INTEGER         IBSET
C
      DO 20 J = 0,NSYM-1
         BITS = 0
         IB   = 0
         I = J
 10      IF (FATHER(I) .NE. NONE) THEN
            IF (I .EQ. LSON(FATHER(I))) BITS = IBSET(BITS,IB)
            IB = IB + 1
            I = FATHER(I)
         GOTO 10
         ENDIF
         CODES(1,J) = BITS
         CODES(2,J) = IB-1
 20   CONTINUE
      RETURN
      END
```

Shown next is the contents of the array CODES for the sample message. Also shown is the array SYMBOLS:

```
*************************************
I    SYMBOL(I) CODES(1,I)  CODES(2,I)
*************************************
```

I	SYMBOL(I)	CODES(1,I)	CODES(2,I)
0	EOF	5	3
1	SPACE	0	2
2	a	4	3
3	e	3	3
4	h	2	3
5	i	3	2
6	s	3	1
7	t	2	1

With this arrangement, ENCODE will first call MKCODES to set up the code tables. For each character in the input file, the array SYMBOL is searched to find its location in the code table. Once the character's location is known, the character's code is looked up in CODES. Below is a version of ENCODE that will do this.

```
      SUBROUTINE ENCODE(IN,OUT)
C Encodes file associated with file unit "IN", and write
C output to file unit "OUT".  Uses Huffman tree for encoding.
      INCLUDE    'HTREE.INC'
      INTEGER    IN,OUT
      INTEGER    I,K
      INTEGER    IB,BITS
      CHARACTER  FGETC,C
      INTEGER    CODES(2,0:MAXNOD-1)  ! Lookup tables

c Make code lookup table.
      CALL MKCODES(CODES)

c Compress file.
      DO 10 K = 1,NC
         C = FGETC(IN)
         CALL LSEARCH(C,SYMBOL,NSYM,I)
         BITS = CODES(1,I)     ! Look up code
         IB   = CODES(2,I)     ! Look up length of code
         CALL PACK(IB,BITS,OUT)
 10   CONTINUE

c Flush last byte, close, and return.
      BITS = 0
      CALL PACK(15,BITS,OUT)
      CALL FLUSH(OUT)
      RETURN
      END
```

This table look-up approach resulted in a good improvement in execution speed, and execution time was reduced from 14.5 sec to 10.7 sec.

At this point a linear search for the location of a character in the SYMBOL array is employed. Refer back to the previous table and note that the array which is being searched, namely, SYMBOL, is in sorted order. A much faster way to search a sorted list is a binary search, so it may be worthwhile to replace the subroutine LSEARCH with the next binary search routine, BSEARCH:

```
      SUBROUTINE BSEARCH(C,TABLE,N,INDX)
C Returns index ("INDX") of "C" in "TABLE". A binary
C search is performed, and "C" MUST be in the table,
C otherwise wrong index will be returned.
      INTEGER    INDX
      INTEGER    N
      CHARACTER  TABLE(0:N-1),C
      INTEGER    L
      INTEGER    U
C
      L = 0
      U = N-1
 10   IF (U .GE. L .AND. C .NE. TABLE(INDX)) THEN
         INDX = (L+U)/2
         IF (C .LT. TABLE(INDX)) U = INDX - 1
         IF (C .GT. TABLE(INDX)) L = INDX + 1
      GOTO 10
      ENDIF
      RETURN
      END
```

When BSEARCH was used instead of LSEARCH, total execution time dropped to 9.2 sec. A binary search is much faster than a linear search, and it seems that one cannot reduce the time for table look-up of the codes much more.

Or can one? Instead of storing the entries in the array CODES next to each other as was done previously, one can store each character's code at a location that corresponds to its position in the computer's collating sequence. For example, with an ASCII collating sequence, one would store symbol t's code information at ICHAR('t') = 116 when the array CODES is initialized. When the code for character t is later needed, the information can be retrieved by looking at location ICHAR('t') in the table. Note that no search is involved. This method is an example of perfect hashing, with the hash function the FORTRAN intrinsic function ICHAR. Below is a version of MKCODES that uses this method, which is almost identical to the original version.

```
      SUBROUTINE MKCODES(CODES)
C Generates lookup tables for compression codes.
      INCLUDE      'HTREE.INC'
      INTEGER      CODES(2,0:MAXNOD-1)
      INTEGER      BITS,IB
      INTEGER      I,J,K
      INTEGER      IBSET
C
      DO 20 J = 0,NSYM-1
      BITS = 0
      IB   = 0
      I = J
10    IF (FATHER(I) .NE. NONE) THEN
          IF (I .EQ. LSON(FATHER(I))) BITS = IBSET(BITS,IB)
          IB = IB + 1
          I = FATHER(I)
      GOTO 10
      ENDIF
      K = ICHAR(SYMBOL(J))   ! Hash function is "ICHAR"
      CODES(1,K) = BITS
      CODES(2,K) = IB-1
20    CONTINUE
      RETURN
      END
```

The subroutine ENCODE must of course also be adapted so that it will work with the new MKCODES, and it is given below.

```
      SUBROUTINE ENCODE(IN,OUT)
C Encodes file associated with file unit "IN", and write
C output to file unit "OUT".  Uses Huffman tree for encoding.
      INCLUDE      'HTREE.INC'
      INTEGER      IN,OUT
      INTEGER      I,K
      INTEGER      IB,BITS
      CHARACTER    FGETC,C
      INTEGER      CODES(2,0:MAXNOD-1)   ! Lookup tables

c Make code lookup table.
      CALL MKCODES(CODES)
```

```
c Compress file.
      DO 10 K = 1,NC
         C = FGETC(IN)
         I = ICHAR(C)           ! Hash function is "ICHAR"
         BITS = CODES(1,I)      ! Look up code
         IB   = CODES(2,I)      ! Look up length of code
         CALL PACK(IB,BITS,OUT)
 10   CONTINUE
C Flush last byte, close, and return.
      BITS = 0
      CALL PACK(15,BITS,OUT)
      CALL FLUSH(OUT)
      RETURN
      END
```

This direct look-up of the symbols' codes reduced execution time substantially, and total execution time fell to 7.5 sec. By performing other optimizations, such as reordering statements in some subroutines, execution speed was futher reduced by about 0.25 sec. Finally, by compiling the program as a medium memory-model program (see Section 5.8) instead of Microsoft FORTRAN's default large memory-model, execution time was further reduced to about 6.25 sec. The program initially took 39.40 sec to compress the test file, so the final program runs roughly 6.5 times faster than the original implementation.

10.15 DECODING

A routine to decode a Huffman compressed file is discussed in this section. No attempt will be made to optimize the program, however, and it is given mainly for completeness. Decoding is done by the subroutine UNZIP, which uses some of the same routines the compression subroutine, ZIP, uses. It is listed below and then followed by a short discussion of the routine.

```
      SUBROUTINE UNZIP(FNAME1,FNAME2)
      INCLUDE         'HTREE.INC'
      CHARACTER*(*)   FNAME1,FNAME2
      CHARACTER*1     FGETC,C
      INTEGER         LC,K,J,IB,ROOT
      LOGICAL         BTEST
      CHARACTER       ID*1(3)
      INTEGER         IN,OUT
      PARAMETER       (IN = 1,OUT = 2)
C Check if input file is a compressed file.
      CALL CHECK(FNAME1)

C Read the header information
      CALL FOPEN(IN,FNAME1)
      READ(IN)ID                    ! Skip over ID bytes.
      READ(IN)NC,ROOT
      READ(IN)(LSON(I),I=0,ROOT)
      READ(IN)(RSON(I),I=0,ROOT)
      READ(IN)NSYM
      READ(IN)(SYMBOL(I),I=0,NSYM-1)
```

```
C Decode the file, and write output to "FNAME2".
      CALL FOPEN(OUT,FNAME2)
      J = ROOT
      LC = 0
      DO 20 K = 1,NC+1
         C = FGETC(IN)
         DO 10 IB = 7,0,-1
            IF (BTEST(ICHAR(C),IB) ) THEN
               J = LSON(J)           ! '1'
            ELSE
               J = RSON(J)           ! '0'
            ENDIF
            IF (LSON(J) .EQ. NONE) THEN
               CALL FPUTC(OUT,SYMBOL(J))
               J = ROOT
               LC = LC + 1
               IF (LC .EQ. NC) GOTO 30 ! Break out of loop
            ENDIF
10       CONTINUE
20    CONTINUE
30    CONTINUE

C Close files, and return to caller.
      CALL FCLOSE(IN)
      CALL FCLOSE(OUT)
      RETURN
      END
```

UNZIP takes two arguments. The first is the name of the input file, which is presumed to be created by the proper version of the Huffman encoding program, ZIP. The second argument is the name of the output file. UNZIP starts by opening the input file and then calls a subroutine CHECK that makes sure that the input file is indeed a valid Huffman compressed file. CHECK does this by examining the identification bytes, described in Section 10.7, in the file header.

```
      SUBROUTINE CHECK(FNAME)
C Checks if the file "FNAME" is a valid
C candidate for decompression
      CHARACTER*(*)  FNAME
      CHARACTER*1    ID(3)

C Read identification bytes.
      CALL FOPEN(1,FNAME)
      READ(1)ID              ! Read identification bytes.
      CALL FCLOSE(1)

C Check identification bytes.
      IF (ICHAR(ID(1)) .NE. 8) THEN
         WRITE(*,*)'Input file is not a compressed file...'
         STOP
      ELSEIF (ICHAR(ID(2)) .NE. 1) THEN
         WRITE(*,*)
     +   'Can only be used with Huffman encoded files...'
         STOP
      ELSEIF (ICHAR(ID(3)) .NE. 1) THEN
         WRITE(*,*)'Incorrect version...'
         STOP
      ENDIF
      RETURN
      END
```

The next step is to read in the file header proper, which includes the Huffman tree, the location of the root node in the tree, as well as the number of characters that is to be decompressed. Decompression then follows, and this is done be reading a byte from the input file, then scanning the byte for set bits. Starting at the root, the left or right child for each node is selected.

This is repeated until the number of bits in the byte is exhausted, i.e., eight children have been selected, or an external node of the tree has been reached. In the first instance a new byte is read from the input file. In the latter instance, the symbol or character that corresponds to the node is written to the output file as a decoded character, and a counter that tracks the number of characters decoded is updated.

Decoding stops when the precise number of characters in the original file has been decoded. When this happens, it is more than likely that an external node has not be reached. This is because a message is seldom encoded into an integral number of bytes, so the compression subroutine ZIP fills the last byte with zero bits during compression; see Section 10.8.

10.16 DISCUSSION

Figure 10.6 depicts how the different optimizations reduced execution speed of the Huffman encoding program. It clearly shows to what extent language extensions, which are the bit-manipulation functions BTEST and IBSET in this case, can have significant impact on a program's efficiency.

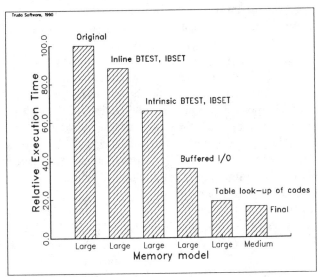

Figure 10.6: Effect of Different Optimizations on Execution Time.

Many times it is possible to implement language extensions in standard FORTRAN, as was done with BTEST and IBSET. In an initial implementation of an algorithm the user-written routines are used in lieu of the nonstandard ones, since this will guarantee portability. If the program is too slow, then use the language extensions. If the homegrown routines are well designed, this is often accomplished by simply removing a few declarations. The user-written versions are of course still available if worse comes to worst during porting.

The addition of buffered I/O routines to reduce hard-disk access time had a major impact on efficiency. It is important to note that the I/O buffers need not be very large to make a major difference, and this technique is largely system-independent. In other words, if buffered I/O increases efficiency on one system it will more than likely do the same on most other systems. In practice, however, some experimentation may be needed to find the optimum buffer sizes.

Another optimization technique, namely table look-up, also paid off handsomely in the file compression program. Because the number of possible entries in the look-up tables were small (the maximum number of entries is not more than 256), it was possible to use a perfect hashing scheme to make table look-up very effective. Combined with the buffered I/O, as well as use of the nonstandard functions BTEST and IBSET, this makes for a fairly efficient program.

There is still room for improvement, though, and one should proceed by again profiling the program. This was done, and it turns out that the modular organization of the file compression program is now the major factor that stands in the way of a faster program. Refer back to Section 10.8 and to subroutine ENCODE, as well as the improved versions of this subroutine in Section 10.14. For each character in the input file, a call is made to the subroutine PACK. For the test file, this means 25,000 subroutine calls.

One can eliminate this by moving the code contained in PACK to the subroutine ENCODE. The same goes for the routines FGETC and FPUTC, and many function/subroutine calls can be eliminated if one still retains the file I/O buffers, but accesses the buffers directly, instead of through FGTEC and FPUTC. How much will one gain by this? One can make a rough estimate as follows. When BTEST and IBSET were coded inline instead of as routines, about 210,000 calls were eliminated. Say all the time saved, 4.5 sec, was due to reduced overhead. This implies that a subroutine/function call takes an average of about 21 microseconds to complete.

If PACK is moved to ENCODE, one can save 25,000 calls. The input file is read twice, so one can save 50,000 references by bypassing FGETC. The program compresses the input file to about 60% of its original size. This implies that FPUT is called about 15,000 times. Thus, one can save a total of 90,000 calls by the suggested optimizations. This translates to a savings of 1.9 sec in execution time. So it is possible in principle to reduce the total execution speed further from 6.25 to 4.45 sec. Whether it is sensible to do this is debatable, for one would lose most of the modular structure of the program and the benefits that results from this. In any event, this is a good point at which to quit the optimization.

Finally, some suggestions for possible improvements to the file compression program follow. As it stands, the program ignores some of the most basic safety rules when working with files. For example, it does not check if an input file exists. Worse still, it does not check if an output file exists, creating the possibility of a user unwittingly overwriting an existing file.

Because compressed files are heavily encoded, an error in a single bit can render an entire compressed file useless. It is therefore a good idea to build in some kind of protection so one can recover at least some information from corrupted files. One possibility is to write a sequence of special control characters periodically to the output file, followed by the file header information. The decompression program will then reset itself when this sequence is recognized upon decompression. Other "bells and whistles" the reader might want to consider include the possibility to add, and also extract, individual files from a compressed file.

11

EPILOGUE

Many optimization techniques, including, among other things, basic DO loop optimization, selective use of FORTRAN language extensions, program generation, table look-up, as well as buffering to improve I/O, have been discussed in this book. Some techniques are contradictory. For example, it is usually faster to use unformatted I/O, so if the situation allows it, this is the preferred method of transferring data. In some instances, however, formatted transfer is faster, and an example of this was given in Section 7.2. As another example of this contradiction, if multiple DO loops are combined, one can obtain significant reductions in execution time because the total loop overhead is reduced. On the other hand, combing loops usually leads to larger blocks of code. On a system with cache memory, this may lead to cache trashing and reduction in efficiency, as discussed in Section 5.3.

A recurring theme in the book is that the effectiveness of a particular optimization technique will often depend on the underlying hardware. A quick look at the various tables in the book will confirm that some techniques may work wonders on, say, microcomputers. The same technique, however, when applied to a program that runs on a VAX, for example, will then degrade execution performance.

When to use what technique is therefore not always clear-cut, and the best strategy may have to be found by experimentation. There is also no substitute for experience. For example, Kernighan and Plaugher [46] say that they

> have found that the best way to avoid too-early optimization is to make a regular practise of instrumenting code. Only from such first hand experience can one learn a proper sense of priorities.

175

An important idea that surfaced many times in this book is that of trading something for speed. Whether one gives up some readability to get a faster program, or spend more time implementing a different algorithm, or use more memory to gain some improvement in efficiency, the basic idea remains the same— buy a faster program with something else.

It is sincerely hoped that it has been shown that programming for efficiency and good programming practices are not mutually exclusive. In fact, programs that implement an algorithm around an appropriate data structure, and on a modular basis, where the modules reflect the basic stages of the algorithm, are usually easy to profile, even with the most rudimentary of profiling tools. Because they are easy to profile, one can quickly find the proper places in a program where one should focus one's efforts.

Detailed knowledge to the last microsecond is seldom needed. For example, when examining the Huffman encoding program of Chapter 10, only a few initial measurements were required to find the time consuming parts of the program, and this guided subsequent optimization efforts. Because optimizations were done in stages, there was little doubt as to what brought the reduction in execution time about. It was therefore easy to get an updated profile, without the (manual) labor of inserting calls to a timing function.

REFERENCES

[1]   Levesque, J.M., *A Guidebook to Fortran on Supercomputers*, Academic Press, San Diego, 1989, 1989.

[2]   Kernighan, B.W. and P.J. Plauger, *Software Tools*, Addison-Wesley, Reading, Massachusetts, 1976, p. 264.

[3]   Ruben, F., "GOTO Considered Harmful Considered Harmful," *Commun. ACM*, **30**(3), March 1987, pp. 195-196, and Readers' response, *Commun. ACM*, 30(4)-30(12)

[4]   *Lahey News File*, Fall 1989, p. 5.

[5]   Bentley, J.L., *Programming Pearls*, Addision-Wesley, Reading, Massachusetts, 1986, pp. 74-76.

[6]   Cooley, J.W. and J.W. Tukey, "An Algorithm for the Machine Computation of Complex Fourier Series," *Math. Comp.*, **19**, April 1965, pp. 297-301.

[7]   Heideman, M.T., D.H. Johnson, and C.S. Burrus, "Gauss and the History of the FFT," *IEEE ASSP Mag.*, 1(4), October 1984, pp. 14-21.

[8]   Rauch, K., "Math Chips: How They Work," *IEEE Spectrum,* **24**(7), July 1987, pp. 25-30.

[9]   Knuth, D.E., *The Art of Computer Programming, Volume 3: Sorting and Searching*, Addison-Wesley, Reading, Massachusetts, 1973.

[10]   Press, W.H. *et al.*, *Numerical Recipes*, Cambridge University Press, Cambridge, 1986, pp. 64-73.

[11]   Angell, I.O. and G. Griffith, *High-Resolution Computer Graphics Using FORTRAN 77*, John Wiley & Sons, New York, 1987.

[12]   Kernighan, B.W. and P.J. Plauger, *The Elements of Programming Style*, 2nd ed., McGraw-Hill, New York, 1987, Chap. 7.

[13]   Bentley J.L., *Writing Efficient Programs*, Prentice-Hall, Englewood Cliffs, New Jersey, 1982, Chap. 3.

[14]   Park, S.K. and K.W. Miller,"Random Number Generators: Good Ones Are Hard to Find," *Commun. ACM*, **31**(10), October 1988, pp.1192-1201.

[15]   Fishman, G.S. and L.R.Moore,"An Exhaustive Analysis of Multiplicative Congruential Random Number Generators with Modulus 2^{31}-1," *SIAM J. Sci. Stat. Comput.*, **7**(1), 1986, pp. 24-45.

[16]   Rabiner, R.L. and B. Gold, *Theory and Application of Digital Signal Processing*, Prentice-Hall, Englewood Cliffs, New Jersey, 1975, p. 367.

[17]   Singleton, R.C., "An Algorithm for Computing the Mixed Radix Fast Fourier Transform," *IEEE Trans. Audio Electroacoustics*, **17**(2), June 1969, pp. 93-103.

[18]   The function ROOT was adapted from *Numerical Recipes*, p. 247, Cambridge University Press, Cambridge, 1986, by William H. Press *et al.*

[19]   Knuth, D.E., *The Art of Computer Programming, Volume 2: Seminumerical Algorithms*, p.442, 2nd ed., Addison-Wesley, Reading, Massachusetts, 1981.

[20]   Wallich P. *et al.*, "Program Notes," *IEEE Spectrum*, **24**(4) April 1987, p. 20.

[21]   Bresenham, J.E., "Algorithm for Computer Control of Digital Plotter," *IBM Syst. J.*, **4**(1) 1965, pp. 25-30.

[22]   Karen A. Frenkel, "An Interview with Ivan Sutherland," *Commun. ACM*, **32**(6) 1989, pp. 712-718.

[23]   Knuth, D.E., "An Empirical Study of FORTRAN Programs," *Software Pract. Experience*, **1**, 1971, pp. 105-133.

[24]   *Guide to Programming on VAX/VMS (FORTRAN Edition)*, Software Version: VAX/VMS version 4.0, Digital Equipment Corporation, Maynard, Massachusets, September 1984, pp. 6-44 to 6-48.

[25]   Dongarra, J.J. and A.R. Hinds, "Unrolling Loops in FORTRAN," *Software Pract. Experience*, **9**, 1979, pp. 219-226.

[26]   The subroutine SCALE was derived from J.J. Dongara's LINPACK routine SSCAL, *LINPACK*, Argonne National Libraries, 3/11/78.

[27]   Larmouth. J., "FORTRAN 77 Portability," *Software Pract. Experience*, **11**, 1981, 1071-1117, p. 1088 .

[28]   Jones, R.K. and T. Crabtree, *Fortran Tools*, John Wiley & Sons, New York, 1989, p. 318.

[29]   Kernighan, B.W. and P.J. Plauger, *The Elements of Programming Style*, 2nd ed., McGraw-Hill, New York, 1978.

[30]   Metcalf, M., *Fortran Optimization*, Academic Press, London, 1985, p. 142.

[31]   Morris., L.R., "Automatic Generation of Time efficient Digital Signal Processing Software," *IEEE Trans. Acoust., Speech, Signal Processing*, ASSP-25(1), February 1977, pp. 74-79.

[32]   Pfeifer, L.L., "Multiplication Reduction in Short-Term Autocorrelation," *IEEE Trans. Audio Electroacoustics*, 21(6), December 1973, pp. 556-558.

[33]   Blankinship, W.A., "Note on Computing Autocorrelations," *IEEE Trans. Acoust., Speech, Signal Processing*, ASSP-22(1), February 1974, pp.76-77.

[34]   Burrus, C.S. and T.W. Parks, *DFT/FFT and Convolution Algorithms*, John Wiley & Sons, New York, 1985, pp .136-138.

[35]   Wagener, J.L. *Principles of FORTRAN 77 Programming*, John Wiley & Sons, New York,1980, pp. 307-353.

[36]   VAX FORTRAN user's guide pp. 1-29.

[37]   Fowell, R.A. and D.D. McNeil "Faster Plots by Fan Data-Compression," *IEEE Computer Graph. Appl.*, 9(2), March 1989, pp.58-66.

[38]   "Erratum: Fowell-McNeil Pictures Mixed," *IEEE Computer Graph. Appl.*, 9(3),May 1989, pp. 84.

[39]   *ACM Algorithms Distribution Service*, IMSL, INC., 2500 ParkWest Tower one, 2500 CityWest Blvd. Houston, 77042.

[40]   Knuth, D.E., *The Art of Computer Programming, Volume 2: Seminumerical Algorithms,* 2nd ed., Addison-Wesley, Reading, Massachusetts, 1981.

[41]   Dunteman, J.,"Is This Angst Really Necessary?," *Dr. Dobb's J.*, 152, June 1989, pp.130-134.

[42]   Foley, J.D., and A. van Dam, *Fundamentals of Interactive Computer Graphics*, Addison Wesley, Reading, Massachusetts, 1984, p. 458.

[43]   *PKZIP* is a file compression program from PKWARE, Inc., 7545 North Port Washington Road, Suite 205, Glendale, WI.

[44]   Sedgewick, R. *Algorithms*, 2nd ed., Addison-Wesley, Reading, Massachusetts, 1988.

[45]   Jones, R.K. and T. Crabtree, *FORTRAN Tools*, John Wiley & Sons, New York, 1989, pp. 49-72.

[46]   Kernighan, B.W. and P.J. Plauger, *Software Tools*, Addison-Wesley, Reading, Massachusetts, 1976, p. 264.

INDEX

%VAL function, 48, 77

Accuracy-speed trade-off, 29
Algorithm
 (see also fast Fourier transform)
 binary gcd, 119
 binary search, 167
 Bresenham's, 36, 57
 Euclid's gcd, 121
 fan compression, 111
 flood fill, 124
 general scan-line, 126
 Huffman, 138
 importance of, 6
 insertion sort, 132
 linear search, 153, 167
 multiplicative linear congruential, 16
 painter's, 34
 Pfeifer-Blankinship, 86
 prime factor, 95
 right-to-left binary exponentiation, 32
 scan-line, 123, 125, 136
 selection sort, 134
 Shell sort, 9
Algorithms and implementations, 6
ASCII collating sequence, 21, 168
Assembly language, 121, 122
 listing, 80

MIX, 119
Association of Computing Machinery (ACM), 116
Autocorrelation, 86
Autogen method, 85, 92
 inline, 89

BACKSPACE statement, 102
Bentley, J.L., 6
Binary
 exponentiation algorithm, 32
 gcd algorithm, 119, 121
 representation of integers, 117
 search, 19, 167
Bisection method, 31
Bit-manipulation, 117, 120
Boolean expression optimization, 61
Brackets, 61
Bresenham's algorithm, 36, 57
 implementation of, 37
Brute force, 33
Burrus, C.S., 95

Cache
 hit ratio, 72
 memory, 46, 60, 72
 thrashing, 60, 73
Caching, 99
 and program timing, 46

forcing of, 46
Character-collating sequence, 20
Code motion, 44, 54, 55
  side effects, 67
Column-major order, 74
COMMON block
  declaring variables in, 78
  passing parameters via, 78
Common subexpression elimination, 54
Compiler options, 4, 14
Computational kernels, 89, 96
Constant folding, 53, 68
Coprocessor, 4, 5, 8, 38, 50, 94, 114
  (see also Floating-point support)
Crabtree, T., 160

Data
  interference, 63
  reduction, 111
  reorganization, 110
Data structure, 9, 12, 128, 141
  importance of, 12
  record, 129, 142
Declaring variables, 78
DFT
  see Discrete Fourier transform
Discrete Fourier transform, 6, 28
  definition, 7
  routine, 22
Disk swapping
  see Page faults
Division, 17, 32, 57
  by 2, 117, 120
  cost of, 54, 56
DO loop, 54, 93
  (see also Loops)
  implied, 106
Dunteman, J., 121
DVPM
  see Virtual memory

Edge coherence, 127, 128
Edge table, 128, 131
EQUIVALENCE statement, 65, 76, 110
  and data interference, 64
Euclid's gcd algorithm, 119
Even integer
  bit pattern, 117
  testing for, 32, 118
Exponentiation
  binary algorithm, 32
  cost of, 56, 62

integer, 56, 62
real, 56, 62

Factorial function, 24
Fan compression algorithm, 111
Fast Fourier transform, 7, 23, 28, 86
  inline code example, 92
  mixed radix, 24
  prime factor algorithm, 95
  radix-2, 7, 22, 23
  radix-4, 23
  radix-8, 23
FFT
  see Fast Fourier transform
File compression, 137
File header, 108
Floating-point support, 38, 40
  (see also Coprocessor)
Flood fill algorithm, 124
Floppy disk, 114
Format conversion, 20, 102, 103, 106
  (see also Run-time formatting)
FORTRAN index, 74, 83
Fowell, R.A., 111
Function
  %VAL, 48, 77
  factorial, 24
  side effects, 65
Functions
  and subroutines, 76
  bit-manipulation, 117, 118, 120
  calculation vs table-lookup, 8
  inline expansion, 115
  intrinsic, 115
  nonstandard, 117
  order of evaluation, 61
  statement, 115

gcd
  see Greatest common divisor
Greatest common divisor
  binary algorithm, 119
  Euclid's algorithm, 121

Heideman, M.T., 7
HPC, 41
Huffman
  algorithm, 138
  code, 138, 139
  encoding, 137, 138
  tree, 138, 139

I/O, 101
  asynchronous, 114

bound program, 51, 101
buffered, 160
data reduction, 111
floppy disk, 106
formatted vs unformatted, 103
system-dependent routines, 114
I/O bound program, 106
I/O buffer, 102
  multiple, 113
  size, 112, 113
Implied-DO loop collapsing, 106, 107, 110, 111
Incremental calculation, 35, 123, 136
  (see also Bresenham's algorithm)
  of squares, 35
Inline code, 14, 58, 77, 88 - 90, 94, 99, 115, 116
  example program, 92
  memory-speed trade-off, 94
  program generation technique, 85, 86
Inline machine language, 115
Inline subroutine calls
  program generation technique, 89
Inline subroutine code, 99
Input/output
  see I/O
Instrumentation of programs
  (see also Profiling)
Intrinsic functions, 115

Jones, R.K., 160

Knotted code, 85, 90, 91, 99
Knuth, D.E., 32, 41, 119

Language extensions, 77, 116, 122
  bit-manipulation, 117, 120
  I/O, 101, 112, 114
  intrinsic functions, 101
Lazy evaluation, 28
Left-to-right rule, 61
Linear
  search, 167
Locality principle, 71
Loop
  combination, 58
  inner, 60, 74, 107
  invariant expression, 54, 64, 67
  linearization (unrolling), 57, 68
  nesting order, 58
Loop overhead, 49, 57, 58, 76

McNiel, D.D., 111

Memory
  -speed trade-off, 39, 88, 94
  caching, 46
  management, 8, 39, 69, 82
  models, 14, 79
  pages, 70
  segments, 79
  virtual, 70, 76
Metcalf, M., 78
Miller, K.W., 17
Morris, L.R., 85
Multiplication
  by 2, 117
  cost of, 15, 28, 32, 55, 56, 98

Nonstandard FORTRAN
  see Language extensions

Odd integer
  bit pattern, 117
  testing for, 32, 118
OPEN statement, 112
Overlay linkers, 72
Overlays, 72

Page faults, 43, 48, 76, 99
  and virtual memory, 70
PARAMETER statement, 54
Parameters
  and subroutines, 76
  passing by reference, 77
  passing by value, 77
  passing via COMMON block, 78
Park, S.K., 17
Peifer-Blankinship autocorrelation, 86
Polygon
  filling, 123
  horizontally convex, 123
  scan-conversion of, 125
  vertically convex, 123
Portability, 8, 14, 18, 101, 114 - 117, 122
Precomputed jumps, 90
Precomputing, 34
Pretty-printing, 111
Prime factor algorithm (PFA), 95
Profiling, 41
  example, 41
  manual, 45
Program generation technique, 28, 85
Programming strategies, 19
  accuracy-speed trade-off, 29
  brute force, 33

flexibility-speed trade-off, 22
incremental calculation, 35
memory-speed trade-off, 39
precomputing, 34
program generation, 28
simplicity-speed trade-off, 20
use of tables, 24

Random number generation, 16
Row-major order, 75
Run-time formatting, 108

Scan-conversion, 125
Scan-line algorithm, 123, 125, 126,
136
Search
  binary, 19
  linear, 153
Shell's sort algorithm, 9
Side effects, 65
Singleton, R.C., 24
Sort
  compare function, 10
  insertion algorithm, 132
  routine, 9, 15, 131 - 134
  selection algorithm, 133, 134
  Shell's algorithm, 9
  using keys, 11
Standard FORTRAN
  see Language extensions

Statement functions, 115
Statement order, 63
Strength reduction, 55, 68
String conversion, 20, 21
Subroutine libraries, 116
Subroutines and functions, 76
Subscript checking, 14
Sutherland, I.E., 38

Table
  lazy evaluation of, 28
  look-up jumps and branches, 98
  look-up method, 8, 24, 28, 39, 57
Threaded code, 85, 90
  example, 95, 99
Timing
  overhead, 49
Turing, A.M., 38
Type conversion, 62

UNIX
  gprof program, *43*
  time command, *43*, 51

Variable declaration, 78
Virtual memory, 70, 76, 83

Wagener, J.L., 101
Wait states, 70, 72
Word size, 14, 17, 70, 79, 80